REDWOOD COUNTRY

and the Big Trees of the Sierra

BY THE SUNSET EDITORIAL STAFF

Editor for this book: Robert Iacopi

Lane Books · Menlo Park, California

ACKNOWLEDGMENTS

We wish to thank all of the many authorities on coast redwoods and Sierra Big Trees who so graciously contributed their time and effort in helping to compile the material for this book and in checking the manuscript. We are particularly grateful for the help provided by Dr. Emanuel Fritz; Norman G. Messinger, Wawona District Naturalist in Yosemite National Park; Frederick A. Meyer, Supervisor of the Environmental Resources Section of the California Department of Parks & Recreation; Richard C. Burns, Supervisory Park Naturalist of Sequoia and Kings Canyon National Parks; supervisors and managers of California's state redwood parks, the national parks, and the national forests; Martin Litton, a former senior editor of *Sunset* Magazine; and the staffs of the Save-the-Redwoods League and the Redwood Empire Association.

Photographers

GEORGE BALLIS: page 80 bottom. CALIFORNIA REDWOOD ASSOCIATION: page 11 top. CALIFORNIA DIVISION OF BEACHES & PARKS: page 62. RICHARD DAWSON: page 41 left and bottom. DAVE HARTLEY: page 43. MIKE HAYDEN: page 23 right. NEIL HULBERT: page 29 right. ROBERT IACOPI: pages 7, 8, 9 top, 11 bottom, 12 right, 13, 14, 15, 16, 19 bottom, 24 right, 25, 27 left, 29 left, 32 bottom, 33, 37, 41 top right, 42, 45 bottom, 48, 49, 50, 52, 54, 55, 56, 58, 59, 60, 63 bottom, 64, 65, 66, 67, 70 top, 72, 74, 80 top, 81 bottom, 83 bottom and right, 84 top left and bottom, 88, 90, 91 left and bottom, 92, 93, 94, 95. WILL KIRKMAN: page 63 top. JIM KOSKI: page 38. MARTIN LITTON: pages 12 left, 18, 20, 22, 24 left, 26, 27 top right, 28, 30, 34, 35 bottom, 68, 75, 81 top, 82, 83 top, 84 top right, 85, 87 right. ELLS MARUGG: page 46, 51. NATIONAL PARK SERVICE: page 73 left. FLOYD OTTER: pages 10 bottom, 71, 91 top right. REDWOOD EMPIRE ASSOCIATION: pages 6, 9 bottom, 10 top, 27 bottom, 32 top, 35 top, 36, 44, 45 top. SAVE-THE-REDWOODS LEAGUE: pages 19 top, 57. DAVID SWANLUND: page 40. FRANK J. THOMAS: page 86. HAROLD WEAVER: pages 77, 79. R. WENKAM: page 87 left. JOSEPH F. WILLIAMSON: pages 70 bottom, 73 right, 76. DOUG WILSON: page 23 left.

FRONT COVER: Eel River in Humboldt Redwoods State Park; photograph by Martin Litton. BACK COVER: Roaring Camp and Big Trees Railroad adjacent to Henry Cowell Redwoods State Park; photograph by Jack McDowell.

CONTENTS

SPECIAL FEATURES

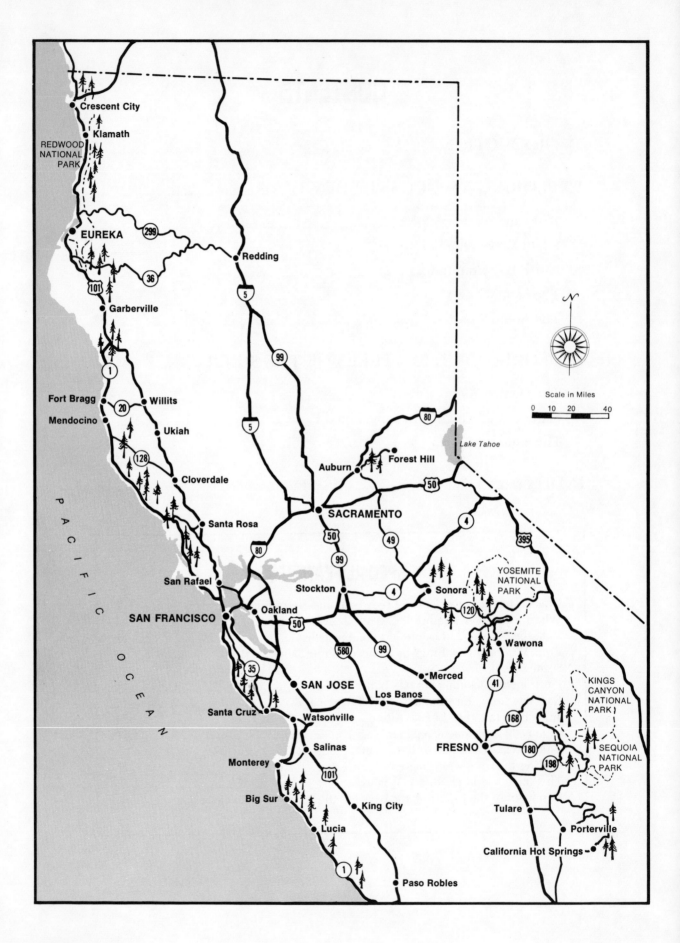

An Introduction to California's Giant Trees

California is fortunate in having within its boundaries two unique and famous kinds of giant trees — the coast redwoods (*Sequoia sempervirens*) that rank as the tallest trees in the world, and the Big Trees of the Sierra Nevada (*Sequoiadendron giganteum*) that are the world's largest living things. The two have some similar characteristics, and in fact, the Big Trees of the Sierra Nevada are sometimes called "sequoias" and "Sierra redwoods"; but key differences clearly distinguish them. In this book, the Sierra trees will be referred to as Big Trees and the coast giants as redwoods.

One important quality shared by the trees of both areas is their ability to enchant and astonish everyone who views them. John Muir wrote about the Sierra's Big Trees: "There is something wonderfully attractive in this king tree, even when beheld from afar, that draws us to it with indescribable enthusiasm; its superior height and massive smoothly rounded outlines proclaiming its character in any company; and when one of the oldest attains full stature on some commanding ridge it seems the very god of the woods."

A similarly glowing description was written of the coast redwoods by Poet John Masefield. Enraptured by their mystical quality, he wrote, "They are not like trees, they are like spirits. The glens in which they grow are not like places, they are like haunts — haunts of the centaurs or of the gods. The trees rise up with dignity, power, and majesty, as though they have been there forever . . ."

Because of their unique qualities, the coast redwoods and the Big Trees of the Sierra have become the most famous trees in the world. The huge trunk of the General Sherman Tree in Sequoia National Park and the shadowy fluted columns in Rockefeller Forest on the northern coast have appeared on the pages of innumerable geography textbooks, encyclopedias, and travel guides. Botanists from all over the world have studied the trees and written hundreds of scientific papers about their remarkable size, age, and growth characteristics. Popular writers have vied with one another with philosophic, poetic, and sometimes inaccurate descriptions of the redwoods and their history.

Even with all this advance publicity, few first-time visitors to these giants are disappointed. To walk for the first time in the quiet of a coast redwood forest, or to come unexpectedly on a solitary Big Tree standing like some ageless sentinel on a Sierra slope, is an unforgettable experience. The trees with the greatest dimensions are irresistible magnets, and it is the rare visitor who can overcome the urge to touch the massive trunks.

Both kinds of trees have a number of unusual characteristics—extreme longevity; remarkable resistance to disease, insects, and fire; self-healing powers—that are fascinating even to laymen. Fortunately, the areas where the trees are found are very accessible. You can walk among the giants, touch them, examine their small cones, and observe their life cycles during all seasons. Many of the best trees are preserved in parks, with informative displays and self-guiding nature trails. Some of the most popular groves tend to be overcrowded, but you can also hike far off the beaten paths and spend undisturbed hours among magnificent giants that even today are seldom visited by man.

How big are the trees?

The coast redwood is the world's tallest recorded tree. The tallest known specimen stands more than 365 feet (see page 28) and there are hundreds over 300 feet. In the days of less precise measurements, there were some claims that other kinds of trees shared height records with the coast redwoods. But now there is absolutely no doubt. Only the eucalyptus of Australia and

*COAST REDWOODS are the tallest known trees.
They thrive along California's northwestern coast.*

the Douglas fir of the Pacific Northwest approach the height of the coast redwood, and thousands of the redwoods are taller than the tallest of either of these species.

The record-holders among the coast redwoods are not irreversibly ranked. The current titleholder along Redwood Creek in Redwood National Park was not found until 1963, and it may be that some undiscovered, unmeasured redwood on a remote river flat may yet turn out to be the tallest. Even some of those that already have been measured may someday grow to heights far beyond those of today's record-holders. The tallest trees along Redwood Creek are only 400 to 800 years old, which means that they may have another five or ten centuries of growing to do yet. Barring accident —and there is a wind hazard in this river canyon—one of these trees may approach 400 feet. On the other hand, one lightning bolt can blast several feet off the top of a tall tree and drop it several notches in the standings.

A few of the mature coast redwoods have diameters of 20 feet at breast height (4.5 feet above the ground), but the average is under 10. Diameter and height are not directly related, so that a 300-foot giant may be only 10 feet in diameter, while much thicker trees rise barely above 275 feet.

The Big Trees of the Sierra have the greatest total bulk — cubic feet of wood — of any known trees in the world. They are surpassed in height by the coast redwoods and a few others, and in diameter by a Mexican tule cypress (which may be several trees that have grown together). But the taller trees tend to be slender, and the tule cypress is only about 130 feet tall, so none can compare with the Big Trees in overall bulk.

With a height of 272 feet, a diameter of 30 feet at chest level, and a total trunk volume of about 50,000 cubic feet (including bark), the General Sherman Tree is generally acknowledged to be the world's largest living thing. But there are several trees with similar statistics, so that very detailed measurements are required to select the "biggest" from a forest of very big trees. These trees are also growing vigorously, so that the measurements require occasional updating.

Measurements of circumference and diameter of redwood trees must be accompanied by the height at which the measurement is taken. The Big Trees, in particular, are characterized by bases that are much larger than the trunk. These massive buttresses are sometimes measured to come up with staggering statistics, but more realistic figures are the result of measurements taken above the base.

How old are the trees?

The oldest known coast redwood was cut in 1934 at the age of 2,200 years. However, very few trees ever reach 2,000 years and the average age of old-growth trees is 500-700 years. The Sierra Big Trees are considerably older. The oldest authenticated age of a downed tree is about 3,200 years, and recent research indicates that the Grizzly Giant in Yosemite National Park is 2,700 years old. Several of the biggest trees appear to be about 1,500 or 2,000 years old.

These statistics place both the coast redwoods and the Big Trees among the world's oldest living things. But they do not appear to be *the* oldest. This honor belongs to some of the Bristlecone pines growing in the White Mountains of eastern California, which have been alive for 4,600 years. Strangely enough, the Bristlecones are not noted for their size; many have a stunted, gnarled appearance which is the result of withstanding thousands of bleak summers and cold, dry winters.

There is little, if any, correlation between the size and age of the coast redwoods and Big Trees. Both grow rapidly under ideal conditions — plenty of sunlight and moisture, and a minimum of competition. A young coast redwood can add 18 inches or more in height and two inches in diameter in a single year, and grow to be a 200-foot giant in about 100 years. The Big Trees also are very fast-growing in ideal conditions and can add an inch to their diameter every three or four years. It is estimated that the General Grant Tree in Kings Canyon National Park — the second largest of the Big Trees — is only 1,800 years old and still growing. A Big Tree cut in the 1850's reportedly was larger than the General Sherman Tree but was only 1,256 years old.

When light and moisture decrease and the competition for the nutrients increases, the growth rate slows drastically. Young coast redwoods that are crowded close together in the shade of their parents may be only an inch in diameter at age 30. There are some 50-year-old Big Trees in Sequoia National Park that are less than two inches in diameter. The growth rate often varies tremendously in the life of a single tree. Cross-sections of cut coast redwoods show clearly that the growth rings can be very thin during the early years while the sapling competes with its brothers, but then increase considerably if the tree suddenly starts receiving more light, either because it finally tops the surrounding forest or loses some of its competition.

Many experts believe that the coast redwoods and Big Trees that have been topped naturally by storms or lightning have the best chance for a long life. Under normal conditions, the trees eventually reach a height and weight that is too much of a burden for the shallow root systems, and they become easy prey for windstorms or topple over of their own accord. This is a major cause of death among these trees, and many a beautiful and otherwise healthy specimen has fallen victim to its own size, particularly if the ground around the trunk has been softened by rain or undercut by stream erosion. But a tree that has its top shattered or knocked off completely is less likely to fall. Its symmetry may be ruined and it may never rank among the tallest of the species, but it definitely has a better chance of surviving. The biggest of the Big Trees are usually those with shattered tops, and the oldest known coast redwood was considerably less than 300 feet tall when cut.

BIG TREES have massive red trunks, rounded crowns, grow only on western slopes of the Sierra Nevada.

THE TALLEST of the coast redwoods are those that grow along Redwood Creek in Redwood National Park.

Where do they grow?

The coast redwoods and Big Trees never grow naturally in the same place. Coast redwoods are restricted to a 500-mile-long broken belt that never extends more than 30 miles in from the ocean (see map on page 4). The Big Trees grow naturally only on the western slope of the Sierra Nevada.

The coast redwoods like plenty of rain, moderate temperatures, and summer fogs. Rainfall is 80 to 100 inches a year in the areas of best development, and while heavy summer rains may be scarce, humidity remains high throughout the year. The Big Trees take more extremes, and may endure 90-degree temperatures in summer and then stand in deep snow banks in the winter. They rarely have any fog, and often go a full summer without any significant rainfall.

The general pattern of growth also is quite different. The coast redwoods grow in a fairly continuous belt, so you can drive or hike through miles of redwood forest. The Big Trees occur only in isolated groves that are clearly defined and often widely separated.

These strict limitations on natural range do not mean that the trees won't grow in other places. You'll find Big Trees planted as novelties in the coast redwood parks, and both trees are often seen in city parks and private gardens in many parts of the West. Coast redwoods have been planted successfully in England, Australia, southern Asia, and South America. The Big Trees of the Sierra do very well in England and Europe.

Natural history

The coast redwoods (*Sequoia sempervirens*) and Big Trees (*Sequoiadendron giganteum*) belong to the family *Taxodiaceae*, which also includes the bald cypress of the southeastern United States, the Mexican cypress, Japanese cryptomeria, umbrella pine, and several other genera that are native to the Far East.

The oldest fossils of this family date back more than 100 million years, and it appears that ancestors of California's present-day giants were widespread throughout the northern hemisphere about 25 million years ago. Fossils of the trees have been found in Germany, France, Greenland, Siberia, England, central Asia, Japan, and many parts of the United States.

The Petrified Forest, about 50 miles north of San Francisco, is made up of primitive ancestors of the present-day redwoods. The trees were buried in volcanic ash from an eruption of Mount St. Helena about five million years ago. One of these fossilized trees is 10 feet in diameter.

Long-term changes in the earth's climate and topography have caused the redwoods and the Big Trees of the Sierra to retreat into the small areas they now occupy. The ranges of the trees do not seem to be shrinking or expanding, and probably haven't changed since the last Ice Age.

In 1944, trees were found in central China that were identical to fossils of a deciduous tree that was thought to be extinct for 20 million years. This is the *Metasequoia*, a distant relative of the California redwoods. The tree is sometimes called the "Dawn redwood" but this term is misleading and is not used by reliable botanists. Because of the great interest in the *Metasequoia*, several have been planted as novelties in the California redwood parks, so you can compare these "living fossils" with the present redwoods.

Discovery of the trees

The first white men to see the coast redwoods were members of the Portola expedition (see page 50). Fray Juan Crespi was diarist for this expedition, and he recorded that on October 10, 1769, while marching near the Pajaro River, the soldiers traveled "over plains and low hills, well forested with very high trees of a red color, not known to us. They have a very different leaf from cedars, and although the wood resembles cedar somewhat in color, it is very different, and has not the same odor; moreover, the wood of the trees that we have found is very brittle. In this region there is great abundance of these trees and because none of the expedition recognizes them, they are named redwood for their color."

The discovery of the Big Trees of the Sierra is generally credited to members of the Joseph R. Walker exploration party which crossed the Sierra Nevada in 1833. Zenas Leonard was the diarist in this case, and his entry reads: "In the last two days' travelling we have found some trees of the Redwood species incredibly large — some of which would measure from 16 to 18 fathom (96 to 108 feet) round the trunk at the height of a man's head from the ground." It is not known exactly which trees Leonard was describing, but it is assumed that they are now included in either the Tuolumne or Merced Grove in Yosemite National Park. Leonard's writings were not published for many years, so the public was not aware of the Big Trees until 1852, when the Calaveras Grove was found (page 63).

The naming of the trees

The naming of the trees is a complicated story, and one that can be confusing to laymen who are not familiar with botanical practices and prejudices. The coast redwoods received their first detailed study in 1794, when English botanist Archibald Menzies collected some specimens while traveling with explorer George Vancouver. He took them home for analysis in the following year, but for some reason, no botanical paper on the subject was published until 1824, when A. B. Lambert described the now-familiar characteristics and named the tree *Taxodium sempervirens*.

Lambert recognized that the coast redwood was a relative of the bald cypress (*Taxodium distichum*) of the southeastern United States and added the *sempervirens* to distinguish the new species as an evergreen, in contrast to its deciduous relatives. *Sempervirens* sometimes is interpreted to mean "everliving" but there is little doubt that Lambert intended it merely to mean "evergreen."

The next botanist to deal with the coast redwoods was Austrian Stephen Endlicher, who reasoned in 1847 that the tree actually represented a genus different from *Taxodium* and really deserved another name. He selected *Sequoia*, presumably in honor of the Cherokee Indian Sequoyah (see page 57), and retained the *sempervirens*. Thus evolved the final and official name of *Sequoia sempervirens*.

English botanists also were the first to analyze the Big Trees of the Sierra. The first specimens were collected in 1852 and taken to England by William Lobb. John Lindley made the analysis and decided that the tree represented a new genus, which he named *Wellingtonia* in honor of the Duke of Wellington. *Gigantea* was selected as the species name in honor of the tree's great size.

The first botanist to recognize *Wellingtonia gigantea* as a member of the redwood genus was Frenchman

METASEQUOIA of China, sometimes called "Dawn Redwood," has been successfully planted in California.

FOSSILIZED ANCESTORS of redwoods and Big Trees are found in Petrified Forest north of San Francisco.

AXMEN OF THE 1890's used saws to make the forecut in a massive coast redwood, axes for the deep cut.

IN MOUNTAIN HOME FOREST in 1877, woodcutters stand on stump of tree cut for traveling exhibit.

Joseph Decaisne. In 1854, he renamed the tree *Sequoia gigantea*. Meanwhile, American botanists were doing some work on their own and in 1855, they published still another analysis, first naming the tree *Sequoia wellingtonia* and then finally *Taxodium washingtonianum*. These contradictions led to some heated debates, but in the end, most authorities decided that Decaisne had done the most scientific and least emotional work, and *Sequoia gigantea* became the accepted name.

But this wasn't the end of the struggle. Twentieth-century botanists took closer looks at the coast and Sierra trees and found that the two differed more than earlier scientists had realized. American John T. Buchholtz finally concluded that the two honestly could not be classified together in the same genus and in 1939, he renamed the Sierra tree as *Sequoiadendron giganteum*. This name is used in scientific circles today, but it has never found its way into public usage, and you'll never hear anyone referring to a Sierra Big Tree as a "giant *Sequoiadendron*," or to Sequoia National Park as Sequoiadendron National Park.

Early logging

Both the redwoods and the Big Trees have been logged, but not to the same extent or degree of success. Logging of the redwoods began in the 1820's — just as soon as the state's early settlers realized that the wood was an ideal construction material, that there was lots of it, and that it was inexpensive. After the Gold Rush, lumber was in great demand in the growing settlements, particularly San Francisco, and the reduced forests represented a fortune to the men who could set up sawmills along the coast, cut the trees and mill the logs, and then freight the lumber to San Francisco by schooner. It was tough, hard work, and the first woodcutters couldn't handle the huge redwood trunks; but they learned quickly, and redwood became one of the chief building materials in early California.

The heartwood of the coast redwood is lightweight, straight-grained, and highly rot and termite-resistant. It holds its shape well, is easy to work, and accepts paints and stains readily. Because of the light taper in the trunk and the absence of limbs at lower levels, the yield from a single tree is very high. The cut redwood also developed a reputation for being virtually fireproof, and while this was a gross exaggeration of its fire resistance, it helped increase the demand for the wood.

The importance of the redwood to the early Californians is best illustrated by this statement of Willis Linn Jepson, a noted botanist and great friend of the redwoods:

"The writer of these lines is a Californian. He was rocked by a pioneer mother in a cradle made of redwood. The house in which he lived was largely made of redwood. His clothing, the books of his juvenile library, the saddle for his riding pony were brought in railway cars chiefly made of redwood, running on rails laid on redwood ties, their course controlled by wires strung on redwood poles. He went to school in a redwood schoolhouse, sat at a desk made of redwood and wore shoes the leather of which was tanned in redwood vats. Everywhere he touched redwood. Boxes, bins, bats, barns, bridges, bungalows were made of redwood. It is employed for the manufacture of shingles, for siding, for interior finish, for fences and for furniture. Its lustrous beauty lends itself to the chasteness of interior decoration, its durability to the plain mudsills of houses, sheds, and factories. From the day of coming into this world, from the cradle to the grave, Californians are in some way in touch with redwood . . ."

It is hard to imagine the amount of redwood that has been lumbered. The U.S. Forest Service estimates that before logging began in the 1850's, there were almost two million acres of redwoods growing in the state. By 1965, there were less than 300,000 acres of partially harvested old growth.

Lumbering continues today in the coast redwoods, but it is an entirely different business than it was during the early days, and many of the major companies are concerned with conservation and forest management, as well as making a profit.

Lumber from the Big Trees of the Sierra shares few of the desirable characteristics of the coast redwood. It is just as beautiful and rot-resistant, but it is much less desirable as a structural material. The wood is brittle and fractures easily, and its uses are very limited. Cutting these giant trees was a laborious and wasteful process, and the trunks usually shattered when they hit the ground, so that only a small percentage — often less than half — of the cut wood ever made it to the mills.

But these deficiencies did not save the Sierra's giant trees from the lumberman's axe. A few of the very largest were cut for exhibitions, and by the late 1800's, hundreds were being cut for box factories, shingle makers, and finishing mills. The cutting of a Big Tree was a tremendous achievement (see page 71), but the shortsightedness of the lumbermen overshadowed all other considerations.

Most of the major logging operations of the Big Trees were concentrated between the 1880's and World War I, with some very limited activity continuing until the 1960's. Of the 35,000 acres of trees that existed before the arrival of the settlers, 23,000 acres (about 66 per cent) still are in virgin condition.

Reproduction of the trees

The coast redwood is the only conifer that is able to reproduce by sprouts from buds on the root collar and bole of a mature tree or at the base of a tree that has been cut or burned. This type of reproductive system gives rise to the tree "families" commonly found in the coast redwood forest. Second generation trees sprout from the stump of a cut tree and grow to maturity while the stump of the parent is gradually consumed by fungi

SECOND GENERATION trees sprout from stump of cut tree, draw on mature tree's roots for nutrients.

CLUSTERS of Big Trees develop when several seeds start in the same patch of exposed mineral soil.

BIG TREES tend to be shorter than coast redwoods, but often have 20-foot diameters at chest level.

BRANCHLESS TRUNKS of coast redwoods extend upward to thick crowns which sunlight rarely penetrates.

or occasional small fires. In turn, the new trees may sprout still another generation of saplings. The result is a shallow depression surrounded by growing trees of varying sizes and heights.

The coast redwood also produces many seeds, but this form of reproduction is much less reliable than root sprouting. The trees develop both male and female flowers on the same tree, and pollination takes place during mid or late winter. The cones mature during the following summer, and the seeds start falling as early as September. The peak period of seed dispersal is from November through February.

Because of erratic fertilization of the female flowers, a small percentage — sometimes as little as 5 per cent — of the seeds are viable. And those that are fertile must find their way to mineral soil before they have a chance to sprout. This is often difficult because of the layer of leaves, needles, rotten wood, bark, branches, and other material (called "duff") that piles up on the forest floor. Only where the duff has been disturbed can the seeds find a suitable resting place.

In the best of conditions, thousands of seeds can sprout in a single acre of exposed mineral soil. But the mortality rate of the seedlings is very high. Drought, insects, rodents, and foraging animals all take their toll, so that a substantial number of seedlings die or are killed before they ever reach a height of six inches.

Tests in the U.S. Forest Service's Redwood Experimental Forest north of Klamath (see page 24) indicate that the coast redwoods waste very little time in per-

petuating themselves. In one logged area, the stumps began sprouting before the freshly cut timber had even been removed, and fresh seed that fell into mineral soil germinated within three months of the cutting.

Root sprouts develop much faster than seedlings, because they can draw on the parent's mature root system for moisture and nutrients. A five-year-old sprout may be 15 feet tall, while a seedling of the same age rarely is more than four feet tall. Over several decades, however, the trees achieve the same growth rate.

In contrast, the Sierra Big Trees reproduce only from seed, and it is a haphazard procedure at best. Flowers are borne on mature trees (100-125 years old) in January and February, and the cones mature in about 18 months. The tiny winged seeds are dispersed by wind, water, and squirrels. As with the coast redwoods, the percentage of fertile seeds is very small, and the great majority of those that are capable of germination are caught in the thick layer of duff and never reach mineral soil. Those that do find a receptive piece of ground sprout readily, but the tiny trees are very popular with ants, chipmunks, cutworms, birds, and deer, so most never survive the first few years.

It seems incredible that the Big Trees reproduce at all under these trying conditions, but most of the groves — particularly in the southern end of the range — are managing to perpetuate themselves. Only where men have prevented exposure of the mineral soil (see page 78) is the reproductive process functioning poorly.

FALLEN MONARCH in Yosemite National Park shows shallow root system typical of redwoods and Big Trees.

THICK BARK protects trees from fire damage. Only a very hot, sustained blaze can reach heartwood.

Characteristics of mature trees

Mature coast redwoods and Big Trees have a special character that makes them easily distinguishable from other trees in the forest. Some features such as foliage and bark are easy to recognize, while others require some study and knowledge of the trees' growth patterns.

Absence of lower limbs. You can often stand at the base of a mature coast redwood or Big Tree and look straight up 100 or 150 feet of bare trunk before seeing the first limb. This condition occurs in "closed" forests where the mature trees form a canopy of branches and needles at the top that cuts down on the amount of sunlight that reaches the lower limbs. These limbs gradually die out, and new sprouts are concentrated near the top where there is more light.

Dead crowns. Old redwoods and Big Trees are notable for their dead crowns. Shattered branches, spike tops, and dead wood are commonly seen on otherwise vigorous trees. Some of this damage is caused by lightning and wind storms. But a more common cause is starvation; surface fires can kill part of the tree's cambium and sapwood near the ground and thereby restrict the flow of moisture from the roots to the branches. The topmost branches are farthest from the ground and therefore are the first to feel the restriction. Even if the fire does not damage the trees, the great size of the mature trees may cause the supply lines to get too long, so that the roots are not able to meet the demands

of all the foliage. Again, the most distant branches feel the effect, and they die for lack of nourishment.

Shallow roots. Neither the coast redwood nor the Big Tree has a tap root. The entire root system is spread out in a wide, shallow network that provides the tree with nutrients and also with support. The roots of a giant tree may spread out a hundred feet or more in all directions but they seldom go deeper than six feet from the surface.

The outermost feeder roots are hairlike in size. These fine feeder roots absorb water and nutrients from the surface, and are very important to the tree's longevity. Because of this, many authorities believe that heavy foot traffic around the bases of the most popular trees may be hurting the trees by compacting the soil and killing the roots. While it is true that the trees are very adaptable and undoubtedly adjust to traffic by growing new roots at lower levels or in untrampled areas, there is considerable danger of long-term damage. This is why you will find fences around the most popular trees.

In dense groves, it is very common for the root systems to become intertwined. This adds an extra degree of stability to the trees and decreases the possibility of their toppling in the wind.

Thick bark. The bark of both the coast redwoods and the Big Trees is fibrous, and rather stringy in consistency. It provides a resin-free layer of insulation around the trees that occasionally reaches a thickness of one foot on the coast redwoods and two feet or more on the Big

DESPITE FIRE SCARS, mature redwoods such as this one in Big Basin State Park manage to survive.

Trees. The bark is usually furrowed or fluted on the larger trees, a condition that is caused when the bark splits as the tree gradually adds to its girth.

The soft, spongy bark of mature Big Trees is cinnamon red in sharp contrast to the darker bark of the pines, firs, and cedars that surround them. The denser coast redwood bark is darker, with shades of gray rather than red.

Tests have shown that the asbestos-like bark is very hard to ignite, even with the direct flame of a blowtorch. Because of this protection—and the scarcity of limbs close to the ground—mature trees are often able to survive fires that clear out the rest of the forest.

Fire scars. Despite the insulating qualities of the bark, most mature trees carry one or more fire scars where flame has eaten through the outer layer and attacked the heartwood. Deep scars often are the result of a series of fires—the first one destroys a section of the bark, and each succeeding blaze enlarges the hole. In hilly locations, most of the severe fire scars tend to be on the uphill sides of the trees, where logs, fallen branches, and other debris collect and provide enough fuel to build up the sustained blaze necessary to eat through the bark.

A series of fires can consume substantial portions of the lower trunk of a large tree. But unless the fire completely encircles the trunk, it usually will not cause death. The flow of nutrients and water from the roots to the crown of the tree takes place in the layer of sapwood, the light-colored outer wood beneath the bark.

THE BEST WAY to enjoy a redwood forest is in solitude, far from vacation crowds and busy highways.

REDDISH BARK of mature Big Trees makes them stand out clearly from surrounding forest of fir and pine.

As long as there is enough sapwood left to act as a lifeline between roots and crown, the tree will continue to live and produce foliage and cones. Many trees that have been badly damaged by fire but still continue to live are found in the parks.

A live tree has the ability to heal its own fire wounds by gradually covering them with a new layer of "skin." Given enough decades without further interruption by fire, the tree may completely cover the old wound and again look like a normal tree. Covered scars are commonly found in trees cut for lumber.

Resistance to insects and disease. Redwoods and Big Trees are vulnerable to very few insects or diseases. This remarkable resistance is an important factor in their longevity and excellent health even in old age.

The resistance is due to the presence of a generous supply of tannic acid in the bark and wood. The Big Trees have more tannic acid than the coast redwoods, and it is so strong that John Muir once was able to mix it with water and use it as ink.

There is one species of fungus—*Poria sequoiae*—that does attack the trees and can cause considerable damage to the valuable heartwood. *Poria* gains entry through a fire scar or some other break in the bark, and then slowly eats into the moist heartwood. The resulting brown heart rot has been known to ruin 15 per cent or more of the usable wood in a stand of coast redwoods, not by killing the trees but by reducing the amount of marketable

REPEATED FIRES have eaten 40-foot-high opening in the Clothespin Tree in Mariposa Grove Tree of Big Trees.

NATURE TRAILS in national and state parks help visitors to learn about redwoods and Big Trees.

HUGE BURL juts out from redwood trunk in Del Norte Park. Burls are valued for their distinctive grain.

heartwood. This rot also helps the spread of fire within the trunk. The decay is an excellent fuel for the smoldering types of fires that can burn for weeks after a forest fire has exhausted itself. The spectacular "telescope" trees that are completely hollowed by fire often were softened up by *Poria* in advance of the flames.

Burls and knots. The trunks of coast redwoods sometimes carry warty growths known as burls. These range from fist-sized knobs to great 50-ton swells. The burls are clusters of dormant buds, but their exact cause is not really known.

Coast redwood burls are highly valued for the beautiful grain and hardness of the wood. They are made into coffee tables, bowls, bookends, and other decorative objects that are sold in every town along the Northern California coast. A small burl will sprout if placed in a shallow dish with a half inch of water, and will continue to live for years with proper care.

Sierra Big Trees never have burls, but they do occasionally develop small tubercules. These have no commercial value at all. In fact, the wood of these trees is rarely used for any of the redwood products that are available for purchase. Even many of the souvenirs and artifacts for sale within the groves of Big Trees in the Sierra are made of wood from the coast redwoods.

Exploring and enjoying the trees

The touring section of this book is divided into two sections, the first dealing with the coast redwoods and the second with the Big Trees of the Sierra. Each section has a general introduction, a detailed map, and a guide to the major groves. If you are a newcomer to California country, you might want to start your exploration in one of the national or state parks.

Aided by the displays and self-guiding trails, you can learn to recognize the trees, become familiar with their growth patterns, and learn something about their history. Once you have this experience, you can expand your exploration to the less-frequented areas where there are fewer people. Don't be concerned about finding "something to do" during every hour of your visit. This is a time to relax, to close your ears to the sounds of the outside world, and let the forest restore your soul.

QUICK REFERENCE CHART ON SIMILARITIES AND CONTRASTS OF COAST REDWOODS AND SIERRA BIG TREES

	COAST REDWOOD (*Sequoia sempervirens*)	BIG TREE (*Sequoiadendron giganteum*)
CLIMATE	A great deal of rain (80-100 inches in areas of best development) but rarely any snow. Heavy summer fogs, moderate year-round temperatures.	Warm summers (up to 90°F) and cold winters (down to −10°F). Precipitation ranges from 20 to 60 inches, much of it snow.
AGE	Oldest authenticated age is 2,200 years. A few are more than 2,000, but the average age of mature trees is 500-700 years.	Oldest authenticated age of cut tree is 3,126 years. Oldest standing tree is thought to be 2,700 years old; a few others may be over 2,000 years.
SIZE	Tallest trees in the world. Tallest is over 365 feet; hundreds more are over 300 feet. Average diameter of mature trees is about 6 feet; a few reach 15 or 20 feet at chest level.	Largest trees in the world in terms of bulk. Tallest is 296 feet; average height of mature trees is 250-275 feet. Largest specimens have 15 to 30-foot diameters at chest level; a few have 40-foot diameters at ground level.
DISTRIBUTION	500-mile-long discontinuous belt near the coast, at elevations ranging from sea level to almost 3,000 feet. Best development in northern area; occurs in pure stands on flats and river benches.	250-mile range on west slope of Sierra Nevada at elevations from 8,800 feet down to 4,500 (and rarely to 2,900). Trees occur in definite groves, ranging in size from half a dozen to several thousand. Only 8 of 75 groves are north of the Kings River; best development is at the southern end of the range. Rarely found in pure stands.
DISCOVERY	1769, near Watsonville, by Portola expedition.	1833, near Yosemite Valley by Joseph Walker expedition.
BARK	Fibrous, stringy, but denser than that of Big Tree. Resin free. About 12 inches thick at maximum. Fluted.	Same texture as that of coast redwood, but softer and much redder in color. Usually about 8-15 inches thick, but may reach 2 feet on largest specimens. Deeply furrowed on larger trees.
FOLIAGE	Narrow needles in flat sprays on opposite sides of twig. Similar to white fir but sharp-pointed at end.	Sharp-pointed, short, awl-like scales completely encircling round branchlets. Somewhat similar to juvenile foliage of incense cedar and juniper.
CONES & SEEDS	Each cone about the size of a ripe olive; light brown. Matures in about 6 months. Seeds smaller and darker than those of Big Tree; about 50-60 in each cone.	Each cone about the size of a lime; bright green when mature, brown when dried. Matures in about 15 months. 150-250 seeds in each cone.
ROOTS	Broad and shallow; no tap root. May extend 80-100 feet from trunk and 4-6 feet in depth.	Similar to those of coast redwood, but may extend outward for 200-300 feet.
REPRODUCTION	Only known commercial conifer to reproduce extensively from stump sprouts. Also by seeds.	By seeds only.

EXPLORING THE COAST REDWOODS

The coast redwood belt is about 500 miles long and varies in width from one to twenty miles, with a few scattered groves found as much as thirty miles in from the coast. It is entirely in California except for two small groves in the southwestern corner of Oregon.

The main part of the belt and the best of the trees are found in Del Norte, Humboldt, Mendocino, and Sonoma counties. Farther south, the redwoods get spottier, until at the southern end of the range, in the Santa Lucia Mountains, they are found only along a few of the river canyons near the coast.

Coast redwoods grow very close to sea level in some areas and extend upward to elevations of close to 3,000 feet in a few places. Even though they grow only along the cool coast, the trees are not tolerant of harsh weather. You'll find the best stands on river flats, in the bottoms of shallow canyons, and on the north-facing slopes of hills,

where there is some protection from storms and hot sun and the soil tends to hold its moisture. The eastern edge of the coast redwood belt is very irregular and depends on topography, rainfall, and the reach of summer fogs.

The best of the coast redwoods are preserved in Redwood National Park and several state parks that are all along the Redwood Highway (U.S. 101). You can see thousands of mature trees along good roads and well-maintained hiking trails in these public preserves. But there are also some fine stands in city and regional parks, land owned by the logging companies, and in residential areas.

The parks are busy throughout the summer, and offer informative naturalist programs, nature hikes, and evening sessions. If you're of the persuasion that a family visiting the redwoods ought to have a square mile or so to itself, then plan your trips in the off season. Late fall

THE SPLENDOR of the redwood country is most apparent on traffic-free side roads and quiet forest trails.

can be an exceptionally beautiful time in the redwoods, particularly if you go to the beautiful virgin forest areas in the northwest corner of the state.

The wildflower season along the coast often extends from March until August, but April to June is the best period. There is also a whole range of delicate living things that thrive only in the full and undisturbed forest habitat—saxifrages, sugar scoop, fat and slim solomon, redwood sorrel, and a host of lichens, mosses, fungi, and ferns. A good guide to the plants of the coast redwood belt is *Trees, Shrubs and Flowers of the Redwood Region,* written by Willis Linn Jepson and published by the Save-the-Redwoods League, 114 Sansome Street, San Francisco, California 94104.

Any forest in which 20 per cent of the trees are redwoods is classified as a "redwood forest," so there are often many other trees mixed in with the redwoods. Most notable are the Douglas fir, madrone, and tan oak (plus lowland fir, hemlock, and spruce in the northern areas). Other commonly seen trees include the red alder, California laurel (also called bay, pepperwood, or Myrtle), Sitka spruce, dogwood, cottonwood, and willow.

Logging companies point out potential fire and accident hazards to bystanders in logging areas, and they don't encourage people to visit the areas that are being harvested. You can, however, visit the demonstration forests that have been established by some of the companies, stop and visit the reforestation displays, or visit one of the large mills in the coast redwood belt.

The largest and most accessible lumber mill on the Redwood Highway is that of the Pacific Lumber Company at Scotia. You can get passes for self-guiding tours of the plant on weekdays at the main headquarters in town. Union Lumber Company at Fort Bragg also provides guided tours and maintains a historical museum.

The lumber companies have opened up about 300,000 acres of their private forest lands to the public. A good guide to the private land is *An Invitation to Recreation in the Redwoods,* published by the California Redwood Association and available at many parks and stores. If you have any doubts, stop at one of the main mills beforehand and ask permission. You may need special permits. Company employees on duty at the demonstration forests and other industry display areas during summer months also can be helpful.

There are also some private displays and parks in the redwood country, including the very popular drive-through trees. For 50 cents or a dollar, you can drive your car through a living redwood. Not all of these cuts were made for today's station wagons, pickup campers, and wide trailers, so make sure there is enough room before you try to squeeze through. It is helpful to station someone outside the car to check the clearance.

Some proprietors of private parks and tourist attractions have taken liberties with the descriptions of the redwoods. It is important to keep in mind that the oldest known coast redwood was 2,200 years old when cut in the 1930's. No greater claims have been authenticated.

REDWOODS grow near sea in Del Norte County.

PICNICKERS enjoy quiet of Samuel P. Taylor Park.

TYPICAL of virgin forest in Redwood National Park is this fine stand on Little Lost Man Creek. Unbroken forest mantles most of the course of this stream a few miles north of Bald Hills Road.

Redwood National Park

When Congress created the long-awaited Redwood National Park in 1968, it set the stage for the eventual development of a 58,000-acre preserve, including 32,500 acres of old-growth coast redwoods. But several years will be required before the land transfers are completed and the new park facilities are developed. In the meantime, visitors to the national park area can rely on previously existing facilities.

The nuclei of the new national park are the three redwood state parks—Jedediah Smith, Del Norte, and Prairie Creek—within its boundaries. Many of the best virgin redwoods are in these state parks, which are logical activity centers. There are several other good redwood areas on the land that was transferred from the redwood lumber companies to the national park when it was created. Some of these are readily accessible, but others will remain remote until the national park's network of scenic roads and trails is developed.

Announcements about the new national park facilities will be made periodically as the master plan is formulated and then executed. When you visit the park, check on the latest developments at the park headquarters, at campgrounds, or at local chambers of commerce.

Jedediah Smith Redwoods State Park

In the northernmost part of the national park land, you'll find some of the best of all the virgin coast redwoods. The area near the junction of Smith River and Mill Creek is quite a bit warmer and less foggy than the coastal sections of the national park, but rainfall is high (about 100 inches a year).

U.S. 199 passes through the northern edge of the park, and while there are some magnificent trees along this well-traveled route, you'll enjoy the forest more if you spend some time on the back roads and out of your car.

The best discovery trip in this area is a drive along Howland Hill Road that starts near the southern end of Crescent City, swings through the magnificent Mill Creek Grove of redwoods and connects with U.S. 199. This is one of the most beautiful drives in all the redwood country, and it offers breathtaking views of dense redwood forest.

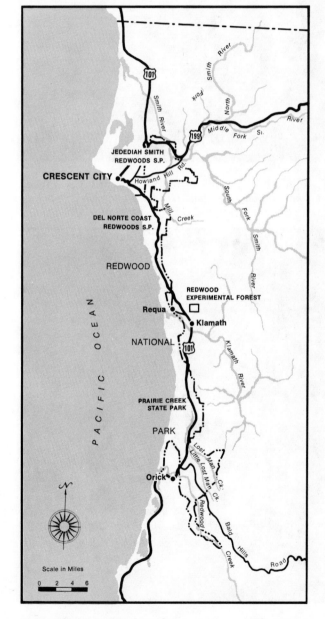

NATIONAL PARK boundaries encompass three state parks that offer complete recreational facilities.

FOR BEST VIEWS of tall trees on Mill Creek, park your car along Howland Hill Road and walk.

STOUT TREE is 340 feet tall, 20 feet in diameter. Base is protected by fence made from fallen redwood.

To make this side trip, take the Elk Valley Road from the south end of Crescent City for one mile, turn off toward the Crescent City Indian Reservation, and continue straight ahead—due east—to where the road winds up a 400-foot rise to Howland Summit. From this high point, you start down an easy grade into the forest.

The road is unpaved and may at first look fearsome to some drivers. But it is a well-maintained route, wide enough for two cars to pass. Its well-packed gravel base makes for secure driving even after a rainstorm.

One of the best features of this side trip is the stillness. There is very little traffic, and you're completely shielded from highway noises. If you take the time to stop and take short walks along the edge of the road, you can really enjoy the solitude and get full views of the giant trees that often form a road-spanning canopy.

When Howland Hill Road finally turns away from Mill Creek, it heads toward the more developed areas of Jedediah Smith Redwoods State Park. Two of the marked trails that start at roadside lead to "Nickerson Ranch," an abandoned ranch in an open flat, and to the Boy Scout Tree, one of the local giants. Near the campgrounds, other trails lead into the Wellman Grove and along the Smith River.

The popular Stout Grove is reached via a short spur road off the Howland Hill Road. The Stout Tree is the featured attraction, but there are many large redwoods along the trail that winds through the grove between the road and the river.

Another loop walk that is worth exploring—particularly if you have small children who tire easily on the longer trails—is the Simpson-Reed Trail north of U.S. 199 about two miles west of the main entrance to the campground area. The trail winds easily through an inspiring grove of trees, and there are several good view points. A fallen log near the end of the trail is thought to be the remains of what was once the tallest tree in the park. On another living tree, a burl has become the base for some maple seedlings.

Fishing and swimming. The Smith River, a fresh, clear stream with all-year fishing, flows through the park. You can catch rainbows and cutthroats in spring and summer, salmon in early fall, and steelhead in winter. The river provides safe and pleasant swimming, with sandbars, a mile-long beach, and deep swimming areas.

Del Norte Coast Redwoods State Park

In this coastal section, you can enjoy a drive through redwood forest right along U.S. 101, take hikes through both virgin and second-growth redwoods, and get a good look at the rugged Pacific shore from high turnouts south of the wooded section.

Del Norte was the last of the northern redwood parks to be developed, and for years it was left only to hikers who were willing to explore on their own and then look for accommodations in nearby towns. In 1967, Mill Creek Campground was opened on the eastern side of the red-

BAIT-CASTERS work riffles of Smith River.

KLAMATH RIVER is placid in September.

WHO'S FOR WINTER STEELHEAD?

Fishing is good in the northwestern counties of California, and many visitors combine a trip to the redwoods with some work with rod and reel. Many of these fishermen consider the top fresh-water sports fish to be the steelhead, an ocean-going rainbow trout that bites and fights fiercely when it is returning to its native stream to spawn. Steelhead range from one pounders to 30-pound giants, and are highly prized by the anglers who wait long hours for a chance to battle one of the fighters. Many of the coastal rivers—including the Russian, Gualala, and Navarro — are favorite streams.

The Russian River, because of proximity to the San Francisco Bay Area, probably attracts more weekend steelhead fishermen than any other stream on the Pacific Coast. The most popular and most crowded fishing spots are west of U.S. 101 where the river winds through redwood forests on its way to the coast. Less popular but just as good is the upper part of the river from Healdsburg north to the junction of its East Fork near Ukiah.

Pool and riffle areas are more widely scattered along the upper river and some of the better fishing locations are inaccessible by car, but this section ranks high with many experienced steelhead fishermen, particularly in the second half of the winter season after steelhead runs on many of the smaller coastal streams have passed their peak. The upper Russian River usually begins producing sometime in December, depending on the amount of rainfall. Generally speaking, the river between Healdsburg and Pieta Creek is easier to fish than the portion of the river upstream from Hopland.

Because its watershed has not been extensively logged, steelhead fishermen can usually count on good fishing in the Smith River even when winter storms wash down mud to render other streams unfishable. And Smith River steelhead average about five pounds apiece, with a few 20-pounders taken each season. Steelhead fishing hits its peak from December through January, though it can be excellent as early as November and may continue through the end of February. Fresh salmon roe seems to be the most effective bait, especially when fished close to the bottom.

Steelhead move into the Klamath River in August or September, moving slowly but surely upstream toward their spawning grounds. The first arrivals are eagerly awaited by an advance guard of steelhead-fishing traditionalists who use only wet flys. The wet-fly season comes to a halt when fall and winter storms begin to muddy the river, but until the waters grow roily, the riffles near Weitchpec and Orleans are among the most popular spots on the entire Klamath for fly fishing.

MILL CREEK CAMPGROUND in Del Norte Park is pleasantly situated in a grove of young alders.

MOSS-COVERED remains of an old railroad trestle are found along Trestle Loop Trail in Del Norte Park.

wood belt where the weather is best, so now campers can enjoy overnight stays in this scenic area.

The campground trail that is best for exploring redwoods is the two-mile Trestle Loop Trail in back of Red Alder Campground. It winds through an area that was logged in 1927. Moss-covered remains of the old railroad trestle, cables, and ties can still be found along the trail, amid the stumps of cut giants and the second-growth redwoods growing among the Douglas fir and white alder. The trail starts near campsite No. 8 and comes out on the main road in the middle of the camping area.

The best virgin redwoods along this part of the coast are reached by the Damnation Creek Trail that starts on U.S. 101 about four miles south of the entrance to Mill Creek Campground, and drops steeply down to a small beach. Between road and water is a glorious stand of virgin redwoods, so magnificent that they make a grand sight even when the trail is shrouded in fog.

The vertical drop on the two-mile trail is 900 feet, so the hike back can be tiring. But this redwood forest is so rare that the extra effort is easily justified. There are many rhododendrons growing on the hillsides, and when they bloom in May and June, the blossoms make a spectacular show of color under the dark redwood trunks.

Rellim Demonstration Forest

The best of the demonstration forests that are maintained for public use by the lumber companies is the

Rellim Forest located just off U.S. 101 south of Crescent City. The self-guiding nature trail passes through a virtual rain forest, with a thick canopy of redwood, spruce, and other trees, and a luxuriant layer of ground cover. The booklet that explains the features along the trail is filled with good solid information about the trees and plants as well as the expected paragraphs about marketable trees and efforts at reforestation.

The Rellim Lodge at the start of the trail is a handsome redwood building; on cooler days, you're likely to find a fire burning in the fireplace. There are displays of petrified wood and cones inside, and the host or hostess can provide additional information on the trail or on the area in general.

Redwood Experimental Forest

The Redwood Experimental Forest just north of Klamath is a federal project, but it is not part of the national park. It is the only federal area where research is being conducted in the harvesting of redwoods and the development and management of new redwood forests.

This is a very special "national forest." Redwoods are logged here regularly, with the encouragement and supervision of the Forest Service's Pacific Southwest Forest and Range Experiment Station. But this is controlled cutting, and the Forest Service is carefully selecting the types of cuts that are made in each section of the forest and conducting long-range studies on the effects of each harvesting method on natural regeneration and the growth and vigor of both the old and new forest. The direct beneficiaries of the studies are the logging companies and other owners of forest land who want to improve their conservation and foresting practices.

A self-guiding tour winds through the forest, so you can drive among the virgin timber and the cut-over areas to learn something about both lumbering and conservation. The High Prairie Tour starts at the Ranger Station at the entrance to the Experimental Forest and covers an area of approximately four square miles. You need not have a map to follow the tour, since it is clearly marked with directional arrows and signs offering explanations of the scenes at each pullout along the roads. The roads are unpaved and narrow, but they are maintained in good condition and will offer no problems to drivers of passenger cars, campers, or trailers. Drive slowly and watch for other cars.

The signs along the roads are uniformly informative and often quite frank in their descriptions. There is no effort to gloss over errors, since this is an Experimental Forest and errors are expected. As a result, you'll see areas that were eroded after they were logged, trees that were blown down by high winds after too many of their companions were logged off, and a fire-blackened section where a fire intended to burn the slash (down wood and top cuttings that result from logging) got out of hand

INTERPRETIVE signs along trail explain tests being conducted in Redwood Experimental Forest.

SAVE-THE-REDWOODS LEAGUE HAS DONE JUST THAT

As you pass through miles of dedicated groves in the state parks—each named for an individual or an organization—you may wonder how these prime fragments of original forest came into public ownership.

To tell the answers in simple terms, these forest parks in the northern coast redwood country exist primarily because the Save-the-Redwoods League has raised millions of dollars (often augmented by matching state funds) to buy the land from private owners and turn it over to the state. The tireless campaign began in 1918, when John C. Merriam, Madison Grant, and Henry Osborn, determined to save some examples of the dwindling redwood forests while there still was time, founded the League. The Founders Grove and Founders Tree in Humboldt Redwoods State Park are named for these men; groves along the highway and along park roads honor donors of purchase funds.

Since its inception, the League's objectives have been actively to assist in the establishment of a Redwood National Park, to acquire for the preservation of scenic values the stands of redwoods along the highways, and to obtain through gift and purchase groves of redwoods threatened by lumbering operations. It has succeeded admirably on all fronts. Through memberships and outside contributions, the League has raised more than $14 million and helped preserve about

50,000 acres of coast redwoods. More than 250 memorial and honor groves have been established in the state park system with League funds.

The League has largely concentrated its efforts in the Jedediah Smith, Del Norte, Prairie Creek, Humboldt, and Big Basin state park areas. League funds accounted for more than half of the purchases that were included in the four northern state parks before the establishment of the Redwood National Park. The League has also helped preserve several smaller groves, and even paid half the cost of the Sierra Big Trees that are preserved in Calaveras Big Trees State Park.

Save-the-Redwoods League was instrumental in the establishment of the California State Park Commission, the State Division of Parks (now Department of Parks and Recreation), and the 1928 State Park Survey. While the Redwood National Park represents a compromise for all parties concerned, it is still the fulfillment of one of the organization's original goals.

Creation of a national park does not mean that the League's work is finished. It plans to continue its efforts to add more coast redwoods to the state park system and the Redwood National Park through private contributions. If you would like to know more about the program, write to Save-the-Redwoods League, 114 Sansome Street, San Francisco, California 94104.

RIVER-DRIFTING family stops for lunch along the Klamath. It's easy to make this "river run" if someone in the party can handle a pair of oars. In summer, the river is warm enough for swimming.

and scorched some of the mature trees left standing.

The Redwood Experimental Forest was created in 1939 purely as an experimental area. It includes 935 acres, much of which is covered with beautiful stands of mature redwood, along with some Douglas fir, spruce, and cedar. Timber has been cut in the forest since 1959. The experiments are not always successful, but they never fail to be interesting.

Prairie Creek Redwoods State Park

Anyone who has camped at Prairie Creek is likely to love this spot more than any other area within the boundaries of Redwood National Park. Not only are there some fine redwood stands, but also the marvelously beautiful creek itself, and the broad meadow where you can stop to observe the band of native Roosevelt (or Olympic) elk that is around most of the time.

Some of the most spectacular scenery in this area is visible to motorists driving along U.S. 101. The redwoods are tall and thick along the roadway, and for miles, you have the feeling that you're passing right through the middle of a wilderness. The entire east side of the state park is virtually one big redwood grove.

Prairie Creek has rain forest overtones. You encounter more luxuriant mosses and lichens than in the state parks farther south, and many of the ground cover species that you find on the wet side of the Olympic Peninsula in Washington. Along with the redwood and Douglas fir

that make up the bulk of the coniferous forest farther south, you'll see Western hemlock, lowland fir, and Sitka spruce. Average rainfall is about 70 inches.

Many of the best trails start right at the Prairie Creek entrance station and branch out into the roadless hillsides. The most popular short hike is a loop nature trail that starts a few yards behind the office and ends up just across the log bridge from the campground. From this same starting point, you can select from among the Elk Prairie, Cathedral Trees, Miners Ridge, James Irvine, West Ridge, and Prairie Creek trails. Rangers on duty can advise you on length and walking times.

To spend a whole day on the trail, you can hike the James Irvine Trail to Fern Canyon or to the beach and back (about 9 miles round trip). You can make a wonderful 12-mile loop by taking the West Ridge Trail north of the camp area, in redwoods all the way, returning on the Prairie Creek Trail which is fairly near U.S. 101 but is still one of the most beautiful in the park.

Two other trails that will take you into fine stands of redwoods are located at the northern end of the park. Little Creek Trail to the Governor Merriam Grove is less than a mile long. Ten Taypo Trail is about two miles long and connects U.S. 101 with the East Ridge Road.

The best back country drive through this area's redwoods is the unmarked, unpaved Cal-Barrel Road that turns east off U.S. 101 just one-half mile north of the campground entrance. It winds up the hillside for about three miles, and you can drive as slowly as you please

A REAL GIANT among coast redwoods, Big Tree in Prairie Creek Park has diameter of 17 feet, 7 inches.

MAPLES, delicately draped with clubmosses, frame picturesque log bridge that crosses Prairie Creek.

among magnificent redwoods that crowd the roadway until you drive onto private land.

Near the Cal-Barrel Road is a labeled turnoff from U.S. 101 to the Big Tree, a real giant that is more than 17 feet in diameter.

Roosevelt elk and a canyon of ferns. By turning west from U.S. 101 on a marked road about 3½ miles south of the park, you can loop through private land and swing north on the pleasantly primitive road along Gold Bluffs, where you can expect to see Roosevelt elk. They will not run from your car and may not run from you, but it is not safe to approach them closely on foot. For a spectacular walk, take the trail along Fern Canyon, where 50-foot-high walls thick with five-finger ferns close in around Home Creek. About a mile up the canyon, you can retrace your steps or make a loop by climbing to high ground and returning to the beach on the James Irvine Trail.

If you drive about three miles north of Fern Canyon, the road climbs steeply back across the hills, through the redwoods, and back to U.S. 101. This is a slow road but allows you to make a loop of your trip to Gold Bluffs.

Other things to see and do. For the fisherman, the lushly grown streams offer native trout and salmon; in the ocean are abalone, smelt, clams, ling cod, and salmon. Several lagoons along the highway south of the park offer boating and excellent swimming. More than thirty-five species of animals inhabit the park, and more than seventy-five kinds of birds may be seen here.

THEY LOOK FRIENDLY, but it's wise to view the Roosevelt elk at Prairie Creek from a safe distance.

NEATLY PRUNED by sea winds, these alders line beach road below Gold Bluff, west of Prairie Creek.

TALLEST KNOWN TREES in the world occupy inside of bend of Redwood Creek shown here.

Lost Man Creek

The redwoods along Lost Man Creek comprise what many believe is the most beautiful remaining virgin redwood forest in California. This was private land before the creation of the national park, so you'll not find any existing state park facilities or even a well-developed trail. A dirt road was constructed parallel to the creek by the lumber company; the turnoff is just one-fourth mile south of the Prairie Creek Fish Hatchery.

Little Lost Man Creek just to the south is another area of outstanding virgin redwoods, but it too was private land until 1968 so there is no trail and you will have to pick your own way through dense slope forests.

The views from Bald Hills Road

This excellent paved road goes east from U.S. 101 a mile north of Orick and stays on the ridge for 18 miles, giving frequent sweeping views across the thickly-forested valley of Redwood Creek and the Klamath River country to the east. The name of the road comes from the grassy balds or prairies along the ridgetop.

In the first mile, as you wind up the steepest part of the road, you'll come to several turnouts where you can park and look south, straight up Redwood Creek.

Before you get to the top of the hill, towering trees hedge you in on the left. You are passing the edge of the unbroken forest that mantles the headwaters and most of the course of Little Lost Man Creek.

The high meadows along Bald Hills Road are fine spots for picnics on pleasant days. As you look west, the sloping foreground woods are splendid, and you can see the ocean or its fog bank beyond the farthest ridges.

The tallest trees

A narrow finger of Redwood National Park extends south of Bald Hills Road to include the world's tallest known trees, on the north bank of Redwood Creek. This grove of giants was measured by the National Geographic Society in 1963. The trees can be reached on a trail that starts on Bald Hills Road eight miles east of U.S. 101— make local inquiries at park service headquarters or at the Arcata Lumber Company mill.

The Glen of the Giants Trail within the grove of red-

FRIENDLY DUCKS try for a handout from picnicking family in Eureka's pleasant, wooded Sequoia Park.

PEWETOLE ISLAND lies just off rock-strewn beach of Trinidad Beach State Park near Eureka.

woods takes you to the tallest (Libbey) tree, the third tallest (National Geographic Society) tree, and the sixth tallest tree in the world. The second tallest tree is in the same general area, less than a mile north of the Libbey Tree and on the same side of the river.

Eureka's Sequoia Park

On a warm day, Eureka's woodland Sequoia Park is a cool haven for travelers. Redwoods, Sitka spruce, Western hemlock, and Douglas fir live together harmoniously in a fine example of the best forests of this region.

Once you've enjoyed the 46-acre Sequoia Park you are sure to return to walk its leafy trails past ferns and streams, to stop at its zoo, children's playground, and picnic area. Fortunately, it's just as pleasant when the day is cool and foggy.

Four beach parks

Although not actually in the redwoods, four state parks along the coast just north of Eureka make delightful stopping places easily accessible from the Redwood Highway. You can picnic at any one of them, but only

Patrick's Point has camping facilities. The ocean along this part of the coast is too cold and treacherous for swimming, but surf fishing is often good.

Northernmost of the four parks is Dry Lagoon State Beach just south of Orick. The beach here extends for about five miles. Sometimes you can find agates or black jade in the sand.

Patrick's Point State Park, with complete camping and picnicking facilities, is one of the most beautiful of all the north coastal beaches. A canopy of big old firs, pines, cypresses, alders, and Sitka spruce shades a thick undergrowth of salal, bracken, and other native plants, and trails lead off into the seclusion of the forest and then emerge on the bluff above the sea.

Farther south, Trinidad Beach Park is one of the most enjoyable spots for beachcombing along the entire Redwood Highway. The park area includes a completely undeveloped, wave-battered stretch of coast, a broad, grassy headland, and an island-studded cove.

Little River State Beach is a good place to dig for razor clams (no closed season, but a fishing license is required). Children like to play in the chilly waters of the Little River, which forms a lagoon before entering the ocean.

ON AN AUTUMN DAY, the morning fog lifts from the South Fork of the Eel River in Humboldt Redwoods State Park. At this time of year, the stream is hardly more than a trickle between quiet pools.

South Fork of the Eel River

South of Eureka, the best groves of redwoods, most of the state parks, and U.S. 101 all stay close to the South Fork of the Eel River. Sprawling Humboldt Redwoods State Park is the main attraction in the area, but there are other good spots for redwood explorers. Several of the smaller parks contain fine stands of old-growth redwoods and are frequently less crowded than the more publicized Humboldt groves.

Grizzly Creek Redwoods State Park

This is a small, peaceful park along the Van Duzen River, highly prized by picnickers and campers because of its climate that is often warmer and less foggy than that along the coast.

There is only one trail in the park. It is a self-guiding one, with informational signs posted along the way. The trail is not one of the best for looking at redwoods, but the signs are a cut above the average and give you a good deal of helpful information about the redwood forest and its inhabitants.

The trail starts between sites 24 and 25 in the campground and swings up into the hills north of State Route 36. There is an extension, called the Hiker's Trail, which goes even higher on the slopes and is generally recommended for those who want to expend some real effort.

Swimming, fishing, and black-tailed deer. Located at the confluence of Grizzly Creek and the Van Duzen River, the park offers both swimming (summer air temperatures are usually in the 80's) and fishing. Black-tailed deer are seen frequently in the high undergrowth.

Humboldt Redwoods State Park

Humboldt Redwoods State Park is the largest of the state redwood parks, with heavy stands of redwood scattered along 35 miles of U.S. 101 between Garberville and Pepperwood. Unlike most other parks, this one has a patchwork outline, but you can explore most of it on U.S. 101, on the 33-mile-long Avenue of the Giants Parkway (old U.S. 101), and on a few side roads.

Approaching from the north, you have at least two entrances to the Avenue of the Giants Parkway and Humboldt Redwoods State Park. If you turn off the free-

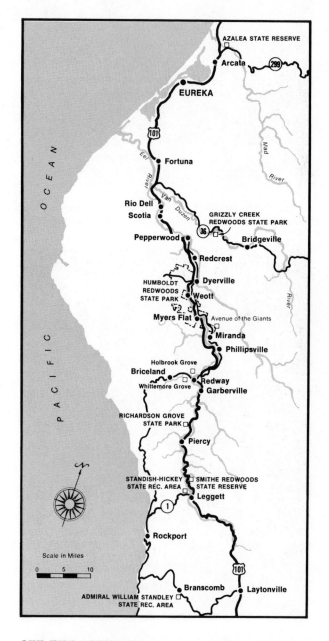

OFF THE FREEWAY, Avenue of the Giants Parkway takes you through many miles of redwood forest.

UPROOTED BY THE ELEMENTS, *a centuries-old redwood tree lies in the magnificent Bull Creek Grove near Dyerville. Many of the stately redwoods in this grove are more than 300 feet tall.*

FLATIRON TREE *has developed a buttress as extra support to compensate for precarious tilt.*

way at Pepperwood, before you actually enter the park, you can visit one of the redwood company's demonstration forests, then start down the Avenue of the Giants Parkway through Pepperwood Grove. Approaching from the south, you enter Avenue of the Giants Parkway 6 miles north of Garberville.

The highlight of the park—and perhaps the finest grove of coast redwoods in California—is the Rockefeller Forest along Bull Creek. To reach this area, turn off Avenue of the Giants Parkway on Honeydew Road which crosses under the freeway near the junction of the main Eel River and its South Fork. You can drive down off of Honeydew Road to a small parking area on Bull Creek Flat. Flood damage within the last decade has reduced the size of the grove, but more than 700 acres of primeval forest still remain. You can just sit under the trees and listen to the silence, or take a leisurely stroll along Bull Creek to see more of the soaring trees.

About four miles west of the Rockefeller Forest parking area is another stopping point along Bull Creek. On the north side of the creek is a short trail to the tallest tree in Rockefeller Forest (359.3 feet high), and just across the river via a footbridge and well-traveled trail are the Flatiron Tree and Big Tree. The base of the Flatiron Tree is 17.5 feet in diameter in one direction and less than 7.5 feet in diameter in the other. This irregular shape develops when a normally-shaped tree begins to lean because of a loss of support on one side due to fire

HIGH-WATER MARK of disastrous flood of December 1964 is shown on sign along Avenue of Giants Parkway.

damage or water erosion on the root system and tries to regain its balance by building out a buttress on the side of the lean. The growth rings get much wider on this side and the round trunk gradually changes into an egg or flatiron shape.

Across the river from the Rockefeller Forest, a side road leads into the Founders Grove and Founders Tree, 364 feet tall when last measured—before about 18 feet broke off in 1958. A short self-guiding nature trail wanders through the forest behind the Founders Tree. Most of the mature redwoods in this grove are more than 300 feet high, and the Dyerville Giant measures 358 feet.

There are dozens of other places for you to stop along the Avenue of the Giants Parkway. There are excellent informal picnicking spots, and every parking area that is bordered by one of the park service's low wooden railings is sure to have a short loop trail leading off into one of the nearby groves.

If you take one of the side roads that lead out to the wide pebble beaches along the Eel, you can get away from the enclosed feeling within the groves and have a long look at the forest instead of constant close-ups of the trees.

Where the Avenue of the Giants Parkway follows the east bank of the South Fork of the Eel between Founders Grove and Myers Flat, you are within striking distance of some excellent redwood experiences that not many

SUNBATHERS and swimmers can enjoy the gravelly bars and quiet pools of the Eel River in summer.

BESIDE THE EEL, along Avenue of the Giants Parkway, thickly branched redwoods screen forest interior.

BEFORE THE FREEWAY, this was main route through redwoods. Much of old road is now scenic highway.

people take the time to enjoy. Because there are more than 60 named memorial groves right along the roadway, not many explorers take the time to park their cars and cross the South Fork to the solitude of the groves on the other side. Those who do, however, can quickly escape the sights and sounds of the day-use areas of the park, and disappear temporarily into dense forests.

Children's Forest is one of the best, and a loop trail starts at the Williams Grove day-use area, crosses the river, and goes a short distance into the grove. Though the trail gives you only a taste of this country, it illustrates the quality of the redwood stands that are preserved in this state park. The Garden Club of America Grove is another area west of the river that is well suited for hiking. Park on the east side of the river just south of Burlington Campground and take the trail to Grasshopper Lookout. Only the hardy will make the entire trip to Grasshopper, since it is 6.2 miles long and very steep. But the first few miles pass right through one of the grandest of all the redwood groves, so you can go just as far as you want and then retrace your steps. Don't worry about doubling back on the same trail—the redwoods

BUILDING THE ORIGINAL *Redwood Highway was an epic achievement. Photograph from the 1920's shows building of culvert near Orick, with new roadbed at top right, above the old county road.*

always seem different with each new view.

The two southernmost pieces of Humboldt State Park are the Holbrook and Whittemore groves northwest of Garberville. These are both small and undeveloped segments of the park land, and serve more as shady havens for local residents than as stops for travelers.

Holbrook Grove is on the east side of the South Fork of the Eel River. The trees are not too spectacular, and the main use seems to be as a picnic site and access area to the water.

Whittemore has more attractive redwoods and even a few short trails. It extends on both sides of Redwood Creek and Briceland Road, and can offer a welcome summer respite when the days get warm in Garberville.

Fishing and swimming. The South Fork of the Eel River, which meanders along the edge of the groves, provides a score of swimming places. During the summer, the river banks are crowded with sunbathers and picnickers. Fishing is good in this part of the river all season, but it is best when the salmon and steelhead are running. Silver and king salmon and big steelhead come up the Eel and its tributaries in fall and winter.

BEACHES *along the Eel are widest when water drops in fall. Crowds are gone; you can fish in solitude.*

A FAVORITE PARK for family groups, Richardson Grove offers stream fishing, swimming, hiking.

BY STANDING ON TIPTOE, boy can span 1,000 years of growth on log at Richardson Grove display area.

Richardson Grove State Park

Richardson Grove is one of the most popular of the north coast parks and has been a favorite family recreation and resort area for years. One of its many attractions is a dense grove of redwoods that shades the main commercial buildings and gives motorists on U.S. 101 a pleasant, if brief, glimpse of tall trunks crowding close to the roadway.

Even though this grove is relatively small, the park authorities have put it to intensive use. There is an excellent nature display, and the short Grove Trail enables you to explore the main part of the redwood stand between the park entrance and the Eel River. A log on display in the nature area is described in *The Story Told by a Fallen Redwood,* an excellent pamphlet written by Emanuel Fritz and published by the Save-the-Redwoods League.

Other things to do and see. This highly developed area offers lodges, restaurants, and stores, both within the park and nearby. There is a gift shop and a post office during the summer season. At several points along the Eel River, lifeguards are provided for swimmers. Fishing is fairly good away from the swimming areas.

Smithe Redwoods State Reserve

Smithe is a small but excellent stand of mature redwoods between U.S. 101 and the Eel River. There are no developments except for rest rooms.

This small stand has two walk-through trees. You can picnic among the redwoods or walk down to the water's edge, where it is sometimes considerably sunnier.

Standish-Hickey State Park

Strictly speaking, this state park is not intended as a redwood reserve. But there are a few points worthy of note. The first is a young *Metasequoia* (see page 9) that is planted in a fenced enclosure near the entrance station. This deciduous youngster has a good start and may someday be one of the most unusual welcome signs at any of the redwood parks.

CAPTAIN MILES STANDISH *Tree stands alone, 225 feet high, in burned area of Standish-Hickey Park.*

WALK-THROUGH TREES *fascinate young visitors to Smithe State Reserve. You can hike to 60-foot waterfall.*

The campground on the west side of the Eel River is in an area where some young redwoods are growing, but there is no resemblance to any of the real redwood groves of the parks farther north. The biggest tree in the area is the Captain Miles Standish Tree, a lonely 225-foot-tall giant that stands in a burned-off area about a mile north of Redwood Campground. A good trail starts between campsites 125 and 126, leads along the cliffs above the river for about half a mile, and then cuts across an area that was burned in 1945. A few mature redwoods survived, including the Standish Tree, but this is generally an area of small second-growth.

Admiral William H. Standley
State Recreation Area

This is a small and completely undeveloped park about 10 miles west of Laytonville. It makes a good rest stop for travelers between Laytonville and Branscomb, but it is really not worth any extra effort for motorists on U.S. 101. The trees are worthwhile, but the road is unpaved for part of the way, and the grove is so small that you can scarcely go for a walk.

CHANDELIER TREE *has opening cut a generation ago; most modern cars can make it.*

ROAD TO PICNIC AREA *in Hendy Woods State Park is shaded by thick stands of second-growth red-woods. Picnic sites open onto a large meadow near Navarro River, which provides good fishing, swimming.*

North Bay Counties

Coast redwoods are preserved in one federal and a dozen state reserves in southern Mendocino, Sonoma, and Marin counties, which were the scene of some of the earliest and heaviest redwood logging in California. California's first water-powered sawmill was built near Santa Rosa in 1834. The first steam sawmill was built near Bodega Bay in 1843. After the Gold Rush introduced great new demands for lumber, mills were started wherever the supply promised a profit. The first mill on the Mendocino Coast went in at Big River in 1852. Even with primitive hand tools, redwood, pine, and fir were cut in great quantities and shipped south by steamers. With the introduction of the circular saw in the 1850's, the mills could handle the bigger redwood trees, and lumbering increased at a rapid rate.

The most popular redwood grove in this area is Muir Woods, the only national monument that preserves the coast redwoods. Taylor and Armstrong state parks also get many visitors because of their proximity to popular resort and vacation areas. In Mendocino county, the miles get longer between parks and the number of visitors falls off rapidly.

Montgomery Woods State Reserve

This is an excellent grove of virgin redwoods, but the park is difficult to reach. The access road is the unpaved Comptche-Ukiah Road, a long route across the coastal mountains. The park is not well signed, so you're likely to go right by it if you're not careful. It is 15 miles west of Ukiah, and just two miles west of Orrs Hot Springs, the only recognizable landmark along the route. Watch for a sign on the south side of the road.

You park in a small roadside area and then walk into the grove of trees. There are some commemorative groves within the main part of the park, but this is mostly a wild area, undeveloped except for a loop trail. The difficult access keeps visitors at a minimum.

Van Damme State Park

There are some redwoods in this coastal park, but they are not nearly as important in themselves as they are to the overall atmosphere of the canyon in which they live.

A narrow road leads up Fern Canyon, a beautiful area of lush vegetation that includes some second-growth red-

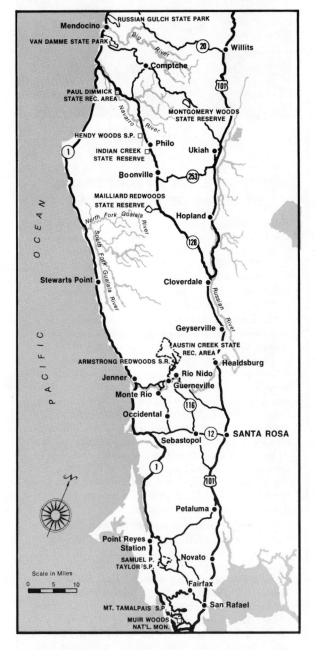

SCENIC ROUTE between U.S. 101 and the coast is State 128. Boonville is largest town along it.

SUPER SKUNK crosses the Noyo River.

FROM WILLITS TO FORT BRAGG BY SKUNK OR SUPER SKUNK

You can make an unusual and exciting tour of the redwood country between Fort Bragg and Willits on one of the trains operated by the California Western Railroad. They follow a twisty 40-mile route along the Noyo River, far from the pavements, power lines, and billboards of the freeways. You get a much closer view of the countryside than you would by car.

The original Skunks were single-car, diesel-powered "rail buses" that performed such routine duties as delivering mail, milk, and household supplies to the few people who lived along the line and providing them with transportation to and from town. The Skunks became so popular with campers, fishermen, and sightseeing tourists that extra trips were added in summer. Then, in 1965, California Western introduced its first Super Skunk steam train, consisting of a 2-8-2 Mikado-type locomotive, a tender, and four Victorian coaches. A second steam locomotive — a saddle tank Mallet 2-6-6-2, built in 1937 — was purchased in 1968. The trip by steam train is a real thrill for youngsters who weren't around in the days when steam engines were the rule rather than the exception.

The single-car Skunks operate all year. The steam trains make a round trip from Fort Bragg every day in summer, and on weekends in spring and fall. Specific dates vary from year to year, so it's best to write or phone before making any definite plans. Advance reservations can be made through the Reservation Desk, California Western Railroad, Fort Bragg, California 95437. The train leaves Fort Bragg at 10 A.M. and arrives in Willits at 12:30 P.M. After a lunch break, it leaves Willits at 2:25 and reaches Fort Bragg at 4:55.

woods with diameters up to about 18 inches. This area was logged in the last half of the nineteenth century and you can still see the stumps of cut redwoods and the remains of some of the old skidroads. The new vegetation is gradually covering the scars. This is an outstanding area to explore by car or on foot.

A pygmy forest. In the southeastern part of the park, you can see mature cypresses and pines growing only a few feet high. This is the most famous of Mendocino County's pygmy forests—an area of shallow acid soil over hardpan, which seems to be the main cause for the dwarfing of the trees which grow there. Pines and cypresses six to ten inches high, with quarter-inch trunks and tiny cones, are fifteen years old; others that are five feet tall have probably lived for a century.

Russian Gulch State Park

Russian Gulch Creek canyon has some good stands of second-growth redwood mixed in with fir and oak. The state park includes about two miles of this canyon, and you can explore it at a leisurely pace.

Coves, tide pools, and a "blowhole." The park lies along the coast just north of the town of Mendocino and extends out onto a wave-scarred headland pocketed with dozens of coves, tide pools, and rocky, surf-battered points. Criss-crossing the headland are many trails from which you can look down a hundred feet into deep-water inlets. Ocean swimming is dangerous, but skin diving for abalone is a popular and rewarding sport. On the headland, about a hundred feet in from the shore, is the "Blowhole," a sea-cut tunnel which has collapsed at its inner end so you can gaze down into a wildflower-lined pit and watch the surging sea below.

Paul M. Dimmick State Park

Dimmick is a "vest pocket" redwood park. The grove of second-growth trees that is preserved is squeezed into 12 acres between Highway 128 and the Navarro River. Virtually the entire park is taken up with camping and picnicking areas, so very little hiking or real exploration is possible. A short self-guiding nature trail winds among the campsites.

The river is a very popular water play area, and the park is likely to be crowded all summer. It is closed in winter, because the river frequently overflows at this point.

The trees themselves are nothing spectacular. Several stumps and broken trunks are visible among the regular growth.

Hendy Woods State Park

Usually given little space in guide books, Hendy Woods is an underrated park. It has the best groves of redwoods of any of the parks along Highway 128 and is definitely worth a visit. It is fairly new, which might account for its lack of publicity and often its lack of campers.

AN EASY HIKE takes you to this waterfall in Russian Gulch Park. Second-growth redwoods are 50 feet tall.

A TINY BOAT is launched on Navarro River at Dimmick campground. River often overflows here in winter.

SCENIC MENDOCINO

For one hundred crooked miles north and south of Van Damme and Russian Gulch state parks, State Route 1 clings to the seaward edge of Mendocino County, dipping and twisting along the craggy shoreline, within a mile of the sea and almost always in sight of steep bluffs, craggy headlands, and rocky little beaches. This is a rugged, haunting country, well suited to the New Englanders who settled it.

The town of Mendocino retains most clearly the flavor of its ancestry. Many of its buildings are hardy survivors of the nineteenth century. Most distinctive example of the early architecture is the old Masonic Hall, crowned by a massive redwood sculpture of Father Time and the Maiden. Mendocino has a highly competent community of artists whose work can be seen in local studios and galleries.

Heeser Drive, on a rocky point west of town, is a pleasant loop road that runs along the edge of the bluff and offers superb views of the pounding surf and wave-sculptured shore. It has turnouts and parking areas, and in a few places you can get down to pebble beaches.

REDWOOD SCULPTURE crowns Masonic Hall.

HIKERS enter dense forest of Hendy Woods State Park. There are two groves of virgin redwoods here.

CAMPERS start a new day in Armstrong Redwoods State Reserve. Campgrounds are usually full in summer.

The virgin redwoods are found in the Big Hendy and Little Hendy groves, both of which are reached by loop trails. But these are not the paved, well-trampled trails of the parks closer to the San Francisco Bay Area. There are just enough signs to keep you from getting lost, and the park authorities have resisted the temptation to name the biggest trees. Instead, there is just the forest, relatively untouched and ideal for aimless wandering and close inspection of the trees. There are two good, uncrowded campgrounds near the groves, so campers can make several excursions into the groves without making a big project out of each trip.

The lack of close grooming on the trails and the absence of named trees may cause some walkers to think there is nothing of particular interest in the Big and Little Hendys. But there are some good-sized trees here, towering more than 250 feet high and ranging up to 17 feet in diameter. As in other parks, there are many fire-scarred trees and many examples of the amazing regenerative powers of the redwoods. You can have the pleasure of seeking them out for yourselves at Hendy Woods, and of letting the children use their own natural curiosity in exploring the forest.

Besides the redwood groves, Hendy Woods has some river frontage that is popular with sun bathers and water splashers. The main picnic areas are in grassy meadows between the water and the edge of Big Hendy Grove.

Indian Creek State Reserve

A small grove along the banks of Indian Creek is preserved in this informal state park. It isn't large enough to warrant serious exploration, but it makes a good rest stop along Highway 128, and you can turn the children loose for a few minutes without worrying about them running through anybody's campsite or getting lost in the timber. No fires or camping are allowed, and there are only limited picnicking facilities.

Mailliard Redwoods State Reserve

Mailliard Reserve protects a very small grove of handsome redwoods in the hills a few miles south of Highway 128. There isn't much to do there, and many families may not feel that the side trip is worth the effort. The trees are easily explored in a short time, and the small creek that runs through the park offers little opportunity for splashing or skipping rocks. Picnicking is very pleasant, provided there is no traffic on the road that cuts through the center of the grove and within a few feet of the small picnicking area. No camping is allowed, and there are no rest room facilities.

Armstrong Redwoods State Reserve

Armstrong Redwoods is a beautiful grove which, like Muir Woods, is hurt by overuse, particularly during the hot summer months when the lower Russian River resort areas are jammed to capacity.

This is an excellent spot to compare the size and distribution of trees in a virgin grove and in one that has been logged. The inner circle of Armstrong State Reserve—the area just north of the Parson Jones Tree that is surrounded by roads—was logged in the late 1800's. The second-growth trees are of uniform size (about 15 to 20 inches in diameter) and are noticeable for their regular spacing.

The virgin timber area—particularly around the 308-foot-tall Colonel James B. Armstrong Tree and the Forest Theater—has the giant trees, the familiar family circles that are part of natural reproduction, and the irregular spacing of the natural forest.

This is a good park for just walking (not hiking) on a trail among the trees. You can't get very far from the roads, so there is no wilderness feeling, but there are enough redwoods of good size to give you a forest atmosphere. The very popular campgrounds and picnic areas are located within the grove.

The Austin Creek area behind the state reserve is becoming increasingly popular with campers and hikers, but there are not too many redwoods, and certainly none that compare with the beautiful stands within Armstrong State Reserve.

To get a good overall view of this area, take time to look at the aerial photographs on display in the park headquarters office.

The popular Russian River

Just minutes away (two miles) from Armstrong Redwoods State Reserve is Guerneville, scene of bustling activity in the summer. This is the center of a river resort area that extends east as far as Mirabel Park and west to Jenner, at the river's mouth. Summer visitors have swarmed to "The River" since the early days of San Francisco, and you'll find restaurants, accommodations, and every kind of resort activity. The river is fairly quiet during the rest of the year, and roads are uncrowded. The steelhead fishermen begin to arrive in November. During the steelhead fishing season (November through February), resort owners and sporting goods stores keep track of the steelhead runs from the time the fish are reported crossing the river bar until they pass Healdsburg upstream. Sportsmen get the word and stand ready at the well-known pools.

Samuel P. Taylor State Park

The fine redwoods in Samuel P. Taylor State Park are only part of the overall feeling of peace and tranquility that makes this a very popular park with residents of Marin County. It is a fine picnicking and camping spot, and more ambitious city-bound families take great pleasure in arising early on a weekend morning and driving to the park to cook breakfast under the redwoods and spend a few hours relaxing along Papermill Creek.

There are some redwoods shading the picnic area between the highway and the creek, but the best specimens

CANOEISTS float lazily at dusk on Russian River. Russians named river Slavianka, "lovely little one."

are on the slopes south of the creek, where they have a northern exposure. Wildcat Canyon is a good place to explore, and the park's self-guiding nature trail leads through part of its groves. Another good trail is the 2½-mile winding route up to the Pioneer Tree. You'll pass through several small groves of redwoods on the way, and the Pioneer Tree itself makes excellent viewing. It is not particularly a giant—in fact, it may not be the largest in Taylor State Park—but its isolated position gives it extra stature.

Mt. Tamalpais State Park

Mt. Tamalpais is a great gathering point for Bay Area hikers. It has 200 miles of trails, some flat and paved, others steep and carved out of the hillsides. They take in both brush-covered sun slopes and shady ravines that are choked with conifers.

Three of the best trails for exploring redwoods are Bootjack, Steep Ravine, and the fire road that links Alice Eastwood group campground and Muir Woods. Bootjack is a steep, scenic trail along Redwood Creek. The redwoods show up only at the lower elevations as you get close to Muir Woods, but the entire route stays in a heavily wooded ravine that is most beautiful after a rain has freshened the water flow in the creek and brightened the foliage overhead.

FAMILY GROUP enjoys a picnic at their campsite beneath the redwoods in Samuel P. Taylor State Park.

Steep Ravine Trail is just that. It drops down the canyon of Webb Creek and takes you through a beautiful stand of redwoods and ferns that live in total shade for a good part of the day. In addition to the trees, there is a succession of ladders, footbridges, and tunnels that make this one of the most interesting trails in the park.

Camp Alice Eastwood is reached on a public road that leaves the Panoramic Highway near Mountain Home Inn. An old fire road drops down from the camp toward Muir Woods and joins the lower section of Bootjack Trail just before it enters the best redwood area.

Muir Woods National Monument

This is one of the most highly publicized groves of coast redwoods. It contains some beautiful stands, and is very close to the population centers of the Bay Area, so that travel writers and tourists can get to it with a minimum of effort. Many glowing words have been written about the cathedral-like quality of Muir Woods and the uplifting spirit of the trees. First-time visitors to the redwoods are sure to be awed by the grove, and San Francisco excursion buses include the grove on their Bay Area itineraries. It's also a favorite with school classes, senior centers, and other organizations that schedule regular field trips. The only visitors who are likely to be disappointed are those who have toured the less crowded parks of the state's northwestern counties, and prefer to enjoy the trees without crowds and paved trails.

Muir Woods is small—about 500 acres—and virtually all of the redwoods are concentrated along the banks of

---

FAR FROM THE MADDING CROWD

One of the most famous of the coast redwood groves is a private preserve owned by the Bohemian Club of San Francisco. Bohemian Grove is located between Monte Rio on the Russian River and the tiny restaurant town of Occidental. But you won't find the Grove marked on any maps or road signs; this is a private place, inaccessible by car and protected against public intrusion.

Bohemian Grove's greatest publicity comes from the annual summer encampment, an internationally renowned retreat that attracts not only members of the Club but also some rich and famous guests, including well-known politicians and show business celebrities. The encampment is off limits to the press and general public, and Bohemian Club members regard all statements and all actions as strictly "off the record."

The party lasts for two weeks, but hits a peak in late July, when there are various forms of lo- and hi-jinks, and the annual Grove Play, written and performed by members, is presented in the outdoor theater.

During the encampment, Club members and guests live in rustic accommodations. But there are enough services and facilities to provide most of the comforts of home. This is a strictly stag affair, and no women ever are allowed into the encampment.

The Club started out in 1872 as an organization for writers, artists, and such. Over the years, it has evolved into more of a businessmen's group, although many members are still practitioners of the arts. The heart of Bohemian Grove was purchased in 1901, and the Club gradually added to its holdings until now it has more than 2,000 beautiful acres.

The land was partially logged until the late 1890's, but a good part of the Grove is in virgin condition. Despite all of their summertime partying, the Club members have gone to great lengths to preserve the beauty of their retreat. Those who are lucky enough to visit Bohemian Grove will see one of the best maintained parts of the coast redwood forest.

Redwood Creek, which cuts through the heart of the monument at the southern end of Mt. Tamalpais. There are some big trees on the slopes above the creek, but most of them were logged off in the early 1900's before the grove was purchased by Congressman William Kent and given to the U.S. Government.

Kent was a Chicagoan who could not bear to see the 300-acre redwood grove go to the loggers. He bought the land in 1903 with his own funds, and then later donated it to the U.S. Government when a water company announced plans to dam Redwood Creek and flood the trees. Naturalist John Muir and President Theodore Roosevelt worked toward establishment of a national monument to protect the trees forever, and in 1908, Muir Woods became an official federal reserve.

Because of a lack of funds to maintain the new national monument, Kent had to spend more of his own money to keep the access road in usable condition. Kent eventually was elected to Congress and played an important role in creating the National Park Service.

The easiest loop trip you can make in Muir Woods is west along the Main Trail on the north side of the creek, and then back on the Hillside Trail on the south side. For a longer, exhilarating loop that gets you higher on the slopes, walk along the Main Trail to the west boundary of the monument, then take the steep Ben Johnson Trail that climbs high above the water onto the grassy ridges, where you can pick up the Dipsea Trail back to the parking area.

The tallest measured redwood in Muir Woods is 236 feet tall. Another has a 13-foot diameter at breast height.

MUIR WOODS is one of most popular of all redwood groves. Main trail follows north side of creek.

SUNDAY PICNICKERS in Redwood Regional Park.

EAST SIDE STORY

The natural range of the coast redwoods is not restricted to the western side of San Francisco Bay. There was a time when the East Bay hills were clothed with thick stands of virgin trees. Some reportedly were so tall that mariners entering the Golden Gate could use them for landmarks. But these trees were among the first to be felled after the Gold Rush, and by 1860 virtually all of the redwood groves were gone.

In the intervening century, the second-growth redwoods have grown rapidly to create a healthy new forest that extends into the residential areas of Oakland and Berkeley and is partially preserved in the East Bay Regional Parks that spread across the tops of the hills. You'll see redwoods in many of these parks, but the best are in Redwood Regional Park above Oakland. The entrance road passes through several stands of tall trees, and there are many picnicking sites beneath their branches. At road's end, the Stream Trail follows a redwood canyon for about two miles.

LOFTY OAKS, madrones, and redwoods shade the broad trail in the middle of the Forest of Nisene Marks. The park includes almost 10,000 acres of coast hills just a few miles from Santa Cruz area.

The Santa Cruz Mountains

The mountain slopes of the San Francisco Peninsula were heavily logged in the decades following the Gold Rush. The first sawmill in the area was set up near Woodside in 1849, and Redwood City was founded as a primitive port for shipping the lumber to San Francisco, Sacramento, and Stockton.

The few remaining virgin groves of redwoods in the Santa Cruz Mountains are preserved in state and county parks, and they can give you an idea of the quality of the original forest that once covered the area. Most of the cut-over areas have had many years to recuperate, so the signs of the lumbering operations are gone and the second-growth forests are gradually covering the slopes with new beauty. You can see these second-growth forests along many of the roads that cut across the spine of the mountains. Skyline Boulevard, Kings Mountain Road, La Honda Road, Boulder Creek Road, and others can provide pleasant driving above the spreading cities.

Methuselah Tree

One of the very large redwoods in these mountains is preserved in a tiny park along Skyline Boulevard between Skeggs Point and Skylonda. The Methuselah Tree has a giant, burled trunk that is 14 feet in diameter at a point above the burls. The shaft rises upward with very little taper to a height of 137 feet. According to the sign near the tree, Methuselah once was 225 feet tall but was shortened considerably by a storm.

San Mateo County Memorial Park

This area was logged of tan oak in the early 1900's, but was purchased by San Mateo County before the virgin redwoods were cut. The park has been developed not only as a preserve for the trees, but also as a popular day-use and camping park. Dozens of campsites and picnic tables are arranged under the redwoods, and facilities are similar to those in the better state parks. There is a fire circle where nature programs are presented, a "swimming pool" behind a dam on Pescadero Creek, and firewood and camp supplies are available.

The redwoods themselves are impressive in numbers, if not size. The largest tree in the park is only 225 feet

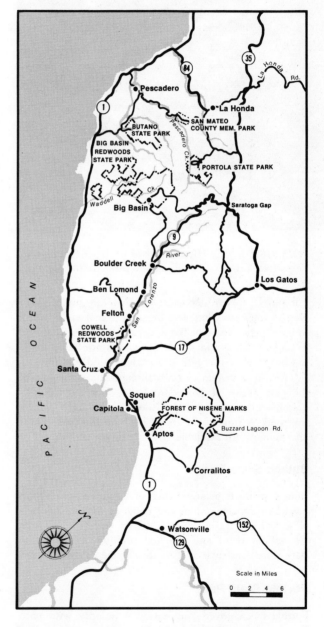

BIG BASIN is California's oldest state park; Forest of Nisene Marks is one of the newest.

YOU FISH FOR FUN more than for record catches in Pescadero Creek. A trail passes through the canyon.

SAN MATEO COUNTY PARK lacks giant-sized red-woods, but has many beautiful trees in campground area.

tall and 13 feet in diameter, but there are hundreds of elegant trees crowded close together to make a beautiful forest setting. Some of the underbrush has been cleared to make room for facilities, but efforts are being made to keep most of the park in a fairly natural condition.

There is a system of trails through the main part of the park south of Pescadero Road, plus a good self-guiding nature trail to Mt. Ellen on the north side of the road. A trail guide and a book on the park plants and animals are available at the entrance station.

Butano State Park

Butano protects a large grove of virgin redwoods, but has always been out of the reach of visitors because of a lack of facilities. In 1968 an access road from Cloverdale Road and the first primitive trails in the park were constructed. More developments are planned.

Portola State Park

Portola has enjoyed long-lasting popularity with both Boy Scout troops who spend a good part of their summers in the campgrounds, and with Peninsulans who

can easily drive up to the park for a Sunday picnic. It has a popular swimming hole, some fair fishing for steelhead, and miles of easy trails.

Redwoods tower over the picnic and camping areas, and a short trail just opposite Point Picnic Area climbs up a ravine to the tallest tree in the park, a healthy old monarch with a 12-foot diameter. But the best redwoods are found west of the main area, on the slopes above Peters and Pescadero Creek. You can hike through these groves on the Iverson Trail, which is particularly good behind the park's Interpretive Center. If you take the Sequoia Self-Guiding Nature Trail, you meet up with the Iverson Trail in one of its most scenic areas.

The most notable tree along the self-guiding nature trail is a dramatic "chimney" tree that has managed to survive a serious fire burn-out.

Big Basin Redwoods State Park

This popular state park is an excellent place both to study and enjoy the coast redwoods. The park encloses a beautiful stand of mature trees, there is a nature lodge with good exhibits, and a couple of short hikes will take you through the best of the forest areas.

LOOKING FOR HANDOUTS, friendly deer look over visitors at Big Basin Redwoods State Park. The herd is a big attraction, especially for youngsters. You're likely to find handsome bucks walking along road.

The entrance roads to Big Basin are a treat in themselves. The eastern access route from State Route 9 passes through a very thickly forested valley that is crowded with redwoods and is a distinct environmental change from the higher slopes. During summer, a thick fog may hang in the lower elevations and enclose the trees in a dripping blanket while the higher hills are swathed in bright sunshine. The main part of the park is at a 1,000-foot elevation and is usually free of fog.

The southern road that connects Big Basin with the town Boulder Creek passes along privately owned redwood lands along Boulder Creek Canyon. This area has long had summer cabins, commercial areas, and private parks, but this doesn't detract from the enjoyment of driving slowly along this popular road and enjoying the trees that flank the pavement.

Big Basin's nature lodge has some of the finest exhibits to be found in any of the redwood parks. There are the usual displays of flora and fauna, plus some excellent and detailed exhibits on redwood growth and on the lumbering techniques used before the turn of the century. Half an hour spent here will acquaint you thoroughly with the life cycle of the coast redwood and will give you a new respect for the men who cut the

SUNDAY VISITORS to Big Basin have a good selection of picnic sites among the redwood groves.

TALE OF THE TALL TREE

The most famous coast redwood tree on the San Francisco Peninsula is not preserved in a state park or hidden away in a sheltered canyon on the ocean side of the Santa Cruz Mountains. It is in the city of Palo Alto, and stands next to San Francisquito Creek, just a few feet from the Southern Pacific railroad tracks and within sight of El Camino Real. The tree is called El Palo Alto (the tall stick) and it has been an important landmark for more than two centuries.

According to local history, the Costanoan Indians, who lived on the Peninsula before the white men, regarded El Palo Alto as a holy shrine, the home of the Great Spirit. They felt safe in the tree's shadow, and held important council meetings at its base.

The first white men to see El Palo Alto were members of the Spanish expedition headed by Gaspar de Portola. They camped under its branches in 1769 while wandering across the Peninsula in a vain search for Monterey Bay. Five years later, Padre Palou, confidante and successor to Junipero Serra, camped by the tree while exploring the Bay Area. He erected a cross on San Francisquito Creek near El Palo Alto in hopes that a mission would be established there. The site was later abandoned in favor of Santa Clara, but the cross remained, to be found in 1776 by Don Juan Bautista de Anza on his exploratory trip to San Francisco.

Fray Pedro Font, chronicler of Anza's expedition, wrote, "...I also noticed that a very high spruce, which is to be seen at a great distance, rising up, like a tower... stands on the banks of the Arroyo de San Francisco." On closer inspection, Font discovered that the tree was not a spruce after all, but a redwood. El

"El Palo Alto" is a city landmark.

Palo Alto evidently was much taller and had a double trunk during these years. But one trunk was destroyed during a storm in the late 1880's, leaving the single top that is seen today.

Because of its prominence, El Palo Alto became a landmark and figured significantly in early nomenclature. Senator Leland Stanford named his new farm for the tree, and the city that developed took its name from the farm.

big trees back in the days when hand tools were still the rule.

Although the park headquarters area may be crowded with picnickers, children feeding deer, and campers checking in for sites, you should begin your exploration of the park's redwoods right here. The self-guiding Redwood Trail starts just behind the Campfire Circle, and it is a good one. There are several unusual trees worth noting—particularly the handsome Father of the Forest, the hollowed Chimney Tree, the disfigured Animal Tree, and the perfectly formed Daughter Tree—and some good examples of the reproductive cycle of the coast redwoods.

For a slightly longer hike through a good grove of redwoods, drive to the far end of what is called N campground (now a picnic area), and then follow the Opal Creek trail to the north. You can make a loop out of this hike by crossing to the west side of the creek (past the site of the Maddock Cabin) and staying on that side for the trip north, then returning on the east side of the

creek. The loop covers only about 1.5 miles, is level and good for children since it requires little effort.

Rangers at the park headquarters can provide you with a trail map and advice on routes. A young *Metasequoia* is planted in a protected area right behind the headquarters building. A slice of a 2,200-year-old redwood is on display on the opposite side of the building.

All of the campgrounds in this park are in the redwoods. There are more than 100 picnic sites just north of the headquarters area and extending along the east bank of Opal Creek.

Henry Cowell Redwoods State Park

This is a fairly large park with 13 miles of trails, but the best of the redwoods are in a compact area near the picnic grounds and gift shop. A self-guiding trail loops about a mile through the big trees. Twenty of the large and more interesting trees are numbered, and you can pick up a keyed guide sheet at the entrance station that

APTOS CREEK splashes over rocks below confluence with Bridge Creek near boundary of roadless, natural area in the Forest of Nisene Marks. Roads penetrate edges of park, but remaining area is undeveloped.

will give you the history and measurements of the numbered trees.

Some of these redwoods are really big. The Giant Tree is 285 feet high and 51 feet in circumference. Among the others are the Roosevelt Tree, the General Sherman Tree, and the General Grant Tree. The Association Group is a good example of clusters that can spring up tightly together through root sprouting.

A small Sierra Big Tree and a *Metasequoia* are planted near the end of the trail, so you can compare their growth patterns and foliage.

First-time visitors to Henry Cowell Redwoods State Park are often startled to hear the piercing whistle and roaring of a steam locomotive working. These are the sounds of the Roaring Camp and Big Trees Railroad, one of the few steam excursion trains operating in the western United States.

Two geared engines (a Shay and a Heisler) pull open passenger cars over narrow-gauge tracks on a one-hour round trip through the redwoods adjacent to the park and up to the top of Bear Mountain.

Forest of Nisene Marks

There are two approaches to this undeveloped state park, which includes a sizable stand of second-growth redwoods among its natural attractions. A narrow dirt road from Aptos leads along Aptos Creek for about a mile and a half. The other entrance is via Buzzard Lagoon Road from Corralitos; this is the better entrance if you want to do some hiking. From road's end, it is about a 7½-mile hike (mostly downhill) through the scenic area of the park to the gate across Aptos Creek Road.

There are a number of redwood stumps 10 to 12 feet in diameter in the park, the results of a period of heavy lumbering at the end of the last century. The lumbermen left a few trees at the highest elevations, and some "mavericks" (double-trunked or deformed trees), and these are the park's only virgin redwoods. The second-growth trees are about 60 years old on an average, and some have already attained a diameter of 4 to 5 feet. Railroad beds from the lumbering days lace the park and you can use them for hiking trails if you don't mind wading through some occasional brush.

THE BEST SIDE TRIP along this section of coast is unpaved county road that circles south from Bixby Creek Bridge. Redwoods crowd close to roadway in some areas, and views are excellent in clear weather.

The South Coast

Virtually every river canyon on the western side of the Santa Lucia Mountains from Rocky Point south to the Monterey-San Luis Obispo county line has some redwoods included in the narrow wooded strips that follow the natural drainage. Some of the canyons are inaccessible, others are private property sealed off from visitors, and others are too small to warrant anything more than a passing glance. The largest of the groves in this area are definitely worth exploring, however, although you will have some steep mountain roads and long trails to negotiate along the way.

Don't expect to find the abundance of virgin redwoods that are characteristic of California's northern counties, but a few of these southerly areas are charming in their own right.

Palo Colorado Road

This signed route—one of the few in this area to carry formal identification—is suitable for both short and long side trips. The first two miles serve the thickly forested Palo Colorado Canyon, where a number of cabins and all-year houses have been built in a fine stand of redwoods. The road is paved but very narrow and calls for slow, careful driving.

About three miles in from the coast, the road climbs out of the canyon and crosses Las Piedras Ridge. There are some redwoods to be seen in Rocky Creek Canyon, but the top of the ridge is open. You run out of pavement near the top, and this may be a good place to turn around if you're not interested in more rugged exploration.

As the unpaved road continues south, it drops down Mill Creek—redwoods visible south of the road—through Bottchers Gap and into the watershed of the Little Sur River. Little Sur forest campground and the Pico Blanco Boy Scout Camp at the end of the road are within this redwood forest. If you want to hike beyond the reach of the road, try the Jackson Camp Trail that generally follows the wooded canyon of Jackson Creek.

It is only eight miles in a straight line between the U.S. 101-Palo Colorado Road intersection and the Pico Blanco Camp, but the road is slow going and you should allow at least half a day for the round trip.

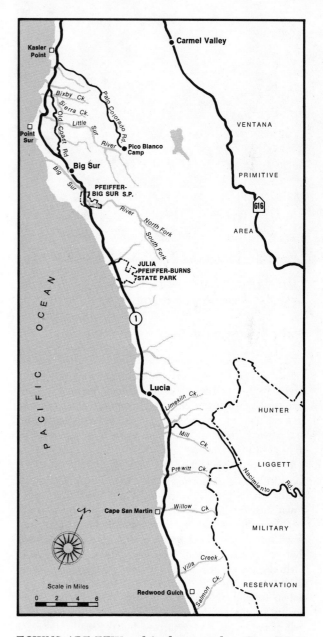

TOWNS ARE FEW and far between along State Route 1, one of California's most scenic highways.

CHILDREN ENJOY making stream crossings on the Little Sur Trail into Los Padres National Forest.

HIGH STUMPS along Little Sur Trail are typical of early logging, when woodcutters started cut high.

Bixby Bridge to Big Sur

A country road (impassable in wet weather) known locally as Old Coast Road circles inland from the Bixby Creek Bridge to Big Sur and provides one of the most beautiful side trips to be found anywhere in this coastal area. There are many fine stands of redwoods, plus magnificent vistas of the coast and the grassy western slopes of the mountains.

If you are traveling south, turn off State Route 1 on the dirt road just north of the Bixby Creek Bridge. It climbs fairly steeply for about a mile and then drops down into the canyon of Bixby Creek and turns south to follow Sierra Creek for 2.5 miles. Once you drop down into Bixby Creek, you are in an area of redwoods that reaches its peak along the banks of Sierra Creek. Virtually all of this is private land so all you can do is look from the road, but there are few drives in the redwood country that can match this one for sheer beauty of the setting and excellence of the trees. The belt of redwoods is very narrow, but the road stays right with it so that you have the illusion of driving through an extensive forest.

About four miles in from State Route 1, the dirt road leaves Sierra Creek and makes its way over the dry Sierra hills and down into the valley of the Little Sur River. The descent into this canyon is the crookedest and steepest part of this side trip and requires some care; but experienced mountain drivers should have no trouble if they take their time.

The beautiful redwoods along the main branch of the Little Sur River are on private property, but the main road continues south along the South Fork of the Little Sur so you are able to spend a few more peaceful minutes under their high canopy.

The Little Sur Trail starts along this part of the road. It is open all year, with special permits required during fire season. The first two miles of this popular route are on private property, and then it enters Los Padres National Forest. The first part is much more than a trail —it is a bulldozed road through an area that was selectively logged in the 1950's. There are three river crossings in the first quarter mile, making this an adventurous hike for youngsters. No fires or camping are allowed on the private property, but you are free to picnic and explore.

Shortly after the trail reaches the national forest land, it climbs out of the redwood belt and crosses the high country for another two miles before dropping back down into the canyon—and the redwoods—near Pico Blanco campground.

When Old Coast Road leaves the South Fork of the Little Sur about seven miles from Bixby Creek Bridge, it also leaves the redwood belt. You'll find a few redwoods in Swiss Canyon and in other narrow stream canyons, but the last part of the trip is mainly one of grand views out over the Big Sur coast. The side road again intersects State Route 1 about midway between Pt. Sur and Pfeiffer Big Sur State Park.

This side trip covers little more than 10 miles but the topography varies from the deep redwood canyons to the bare and windswept bluffs that characterize much of the western slope of the Santa Lucias. There may not be as many opportunities to stop and walk around as you might like, but even a stroll along the road in the deepest part of the forests can be a refreshing experience.

Pfeiffer-Big Sur State Park

This is the center of activity along the Big Sur coast, and the state park includes some beautiful redwoods. The main grove in the park includes the entrance station and extends northward along the trail to Pfeiffer Falls. The rangers lead guided walks along this trail, or you can walk it by yourself in less than an hour. It stays within the redwood forest for virtually its entire length, and can provide a cooling walk on warm days.

Redwoods are also found along the self-guiding nature trail and in some of the camping areas. The nature exhibit area includes a cross section of the 2,200-year-old redwood that was cut along the Avenue of the Giants in 1934.

The self-guiding nature trail is not unusual in its length or commentary, but is especially good for children since it stays on the banks of the Big Sur River where little people can throw pebbles, find "crawdads," and watch for small trout in the shallow waters. Perhaps the most interesting redwood on the trip is the flatiron tree that has developed a buttress to counteract a tendency to lean.

A beautiful redwood forest extends along the Big Sur River and its tributaries that extend out into the Ventana Primitive Area east of the state park. But there is no trail along the canyon, and hikers have to pick their own way if they want to explore the redwoods. The Pine Ridge Trail does cut across some of the redwood canyons on its way east to Tassajara Hot Springs Road across Chews Ridge, but it is primarily a high trail that avoids the thickly forested areas.

South of the state park, you can see redwoods in Graves, Castro, Grimes, Torre, Partingon, Anderson, Burns, Buck, Hot Springs, Dolan, Devils, and Vicente canyons. But all of this is private property, and you must do your gazing from the roadways.

IT TAKES PATIENCE to catch fish in Pfeiffer-Big Sur Park, but these anglers are hopeful.

IN MILL CREEK CANYON, and most canyons along coast, forest is confined to north-facing slope.

A river-fed swimming pool. Pfeiffer-Big Sur has one of the best swimming pools in the state park system—a big, artificial basin with the cool waters of the Big Sur River flowing through it. Sycamores and other native trees border the pool, and the high ridges of the Santa Lucia Mountains form a beautiful backdrop. A lifeguard is on duty during the summer.

Julia Pfeiffer-Burns State Park

This is the southernmost of the redwood state parks. It is twice as big as Pfeiffer-Big Sur, but the huge undeveloped portion of the park is completely closed to the public due to summer fire hazards and a lack of sanitation facilities. Only a small section near the highway is accessible.

In 1968 about 15 picnicking sites were furnished as the first developments at Pfeiffer-Burns. There is only one trail, which winds through a small redwood grove near the developed area.

Mill Creek

South of Limekiln Creek, State Route 1 enters Los Padres National Forest, and the redwood canyons are more accessible to the public. One of the largest areas of redwoods is along Mill Creek, which is reached via Nacimiento Road that turns off the highway near the Kirk Creek picnic area. Nacimiento Road circles deep through the national forest land and then splits in two, with the northern branch ending at Cone Peak and the southern fork passing through the high country and then back down to the coast near Plaskett Creek. But to explore Mill Creek, you need only take Nacimiento Road for less than a mile, then park and hike along the canyon for another two miles.

The redwoods—and the forest in general—follow a pattern in Mill Creek that is typical of this entire area. The coast redwoods thrive along the river bottoms and on the north-facing slopes where they are protected against the direct exposure to sun and the strong coastal winds. Because of this, each of the canyons tends to have one side cloaked in deep green redwood and pine forest, while the opposite slope tends to be dry and open with only a few evergreens and live oaks crowded along the infrequent creek channels.

Prewitt Creek

You can't drive along Prewitt Creek, but you can park along State Route 1 and take a rough fisherman's trail that winds its way about half a mile along the watercourse. The redwoods themselves are not spectacular, but the thick brush and canopy of trees overhead make a pleasant setting for a short walk.

Willow Creek

The southernmost large grove of coast redwoods is found along Willow Creek, inland from Cape San Martin. You can drive in on an unpaved road about 2.5 miles, park where you find the "Willow Creek Campground" sign and hike the remaining three miles down into redwood canyons. For the first mile, you walk along a steep road that is suitable for four-wheel-drive vehicles only, and then start on the trail through the redwoods along the creek. The Willow Creek campground is a small area along the water. There are a few cabins scattered on either side.

At the campground, the trail crosses the main branch of Willow Creek and follows its North Fork for about a mile before climbing out onto Plaskett Ridge. There are some superlative views available from the upper slopes, as you look back down into the dense redwood forest in the river canyons. Both Ponderosa pine and Douglas fir are mixed in with the redwoods throughout this area.

The six-mile round trip can be made in a few hours, but the area is agreeable for all-day exploration.

SEQUOYAH—GIANT AMONG RED MEN

The California redwoods are named after Sequoyah, a self-taught linguist who devised a written language for the Cherokee Indians of North America. The name was selected by Austrian botanist Stephen Endlicher, who combined interests in language and American history with his scientific career, and was thereby able to recognize the resemblance between a giant among red men and the newly discovered giants of red wood.

Despite the fact that Sequoyah never visited California or set eyes on a redwood, he is certainly worthy of the honor of having his name attached to these great trees. He was the first person in recorded history single-handedly to originate and perfect an alphabet. Because of his work, the illiterate Cherokees could learn to read and write without any expense or formal education.

Very little is known about Sequoyah's early life. He was born about 1770 of a Cherokee mother and white father and was raised as an Indian in a small Tennessee village. Even though he had no schooling, Sequoyah evidently became interested in languages at an early age. He realized that the Cherokees suffered because they could not write down their ideas as did the white men, and in 1809, he decided to try his hand at devising some sort of written language.

Fellow Cherokees were not sympathetic to Sequoyah's ambitions, and he was forced to withdraw from tribal life and work by himself. The task was immense. Sequoyah experimented for years with different ideas before deciding that sounds were the key elements of the language and that he would have to divide each Cherokee word into syllables and then assign a written character to each syllable. Writing on bark with a knife or nail, Sequoyah was finally able to develop a system of 86 characters that expressed all the sounds in his language. Some of the characters were adaptations of English letters that he found in a spelling book, and others were pictures and new symbols.

All of this required 12 years of effort. But the job wasn't finished. Sequoyah still had to sell his ideas to his reluctant fellow Cherokees. They were slow to accept it. Many feared him as a witch doctor, and others — including his wife — believed that he had lost his sanity. But Sequoyah's daughter was loyal, and with her help, he was able to demonstrate to tribal leaders how a message could be written in one village and read in another if both the writer and reader learned the same set of characters.

SEQUOYAH, inventor of Cherokee alphabet.

Once the Cherokees realized the value of Sequoyah's alphabet, they put it to immediate use. In 1828, a missionary helped their cause by securing government approval for the acquisition of a printing press and type faces of the Cherokee characters. A newspaper called the *Cherokee Phoenix* was started, parts of the Bible were translated, and Indian history was permanently recorded.

Sequoyah didn't gain much wealth with his alphabet, but he did achieve great stature with his tribe and with linguists of the world. The Cherokee nation gave him a silver medal of respect and admiration, and the U.S. government gave him some gifts and $150 in cash. With his life work completed, Sequoyah retired to a small Oklahoma farm. He died in 1843 while visiting Cherokees in Mexico.

Thus the name of Sequoyah was still fresh in history when Stephen Endlicher first studied the California redwoods in 1847. And it must have seemed appropriate to the Austrian to select the name of America's famous Indian as the name for America's famous trees. Sequoyah was changed to *Sequoia* in keeping with botanical tradition, and the ingenious Cherokee acquired another, longer-lasting honor to go along with his silver medal and $150 cash.

Redwood Gulch

The southernmost spot where you can see coast redwoods along State Route 1 is at Redwood Gulch. They stand silent and gray within a stone's throw of the pavement. A short trail drops down to the creek bed, but the best view of the trees is from the shoulders of the highway.

The most southerly natural stand of coast redwoods is just a few hundred yards south of Redwood Gulch. The trees are not visible from the highway and are not very impressive anyway, so are notable only because they are the last in line.

Many guidebooks report redwoods on Salmon Creek a few miles south of Redwood Creek. There are some redwoods growing along the San Carpoforo drainage south of Salmon Creek, but these trees were planted by the Hearst Ranch and are not a natural stand.

EXPLORING THE BIG TREES OF THE SIERRA

Exploring the Sierra's Big Trees is not quite as easy as exploring the coast redwoods. There is no "Redwood Highway" along the western slope of the Sierra, and the groves are often widely separated by miles of twisting two-lane road. The range of the Big Trees extends about 250 miles. The northernmost grove is in Placer County about 60 miles northwest of Auburn, and the southernmost grove is 35 miles southeast of Porterville in Tulare County.

The Big Trees are not found in a continuous belt. They occur in groves ranging in size from half a dozen trees to several thousand; single trees are sometimes found, but they are rare. There are about 75 groves, only eight of which are north of the Kings River. These northern stands are widely scattered, and although there are some grand individual specimens, the general development is not as spectacular as it is in the southern part of the range, where the groves are much closer together and the trees reach their finest quality. The Big Trees are restricted to elevations between 4,500 and 7,500 feet in the north, but the growth range drops below 3,000 feet and extends up to 8,800 feet in the south. Precipitation averages 45 to 60 inches, mostly in the form of snow.

Big Trees grow best in well-drained soils, but excellent specimens are found on ridge tops as well as on valley bottoms or mountain slopes where there is plenty of underground moisture within a few feet of the surface during much of the year.

John Muir attributed the distribution of the Big

HOLLOW LOG in Balch County Park never fails to attract young visitors.

Trees to the fact that those remaining are the only ones that survived the last Ice Age. He believed that nearly all the Big Trees are found living on non-glacial soils where they were not disturbed by the advancing ice. The gaps in the glacial development were smaller and fewer in number in the north, which is why there are now so few Big Trees north of the Kings River.

The groves do not seem to be shrinking in size. Natural reproduction is better in the southern groves, but even in the northern half of the range, there is no evidence that the groves have changed their present size or shape since the ice retreated.

The Big Trees are never found in pure stands. You'll always find several other types of trees mixed in the groves, particularly white fir, sugar pine, incense cedar, and ponderosa pine. The spottiness of the groves and the lack of density of the Big Trees within the groves is illustrated by the fact that there are only about 2,571 Big Trees of 10-foot diameter or larger in the 2,000 acres of Giant Forest in Sequoia National Park.

Big Trees do not assume their adult shape—thick untapered trunk, red bark, elbowed limbs starting 100 feet or more from the ground—until they reach an age of 75 or 100 years. Until then, they look much more like a conical Christmas tree than miniatures of the world's largest trees. Many visitors to the Sierra do not recognize young Big Trees unless they are signed or are pointed out by one of the rangers. If you learn to recognize the distinct foliage, then you'll be able to recognize the one-foot-tall Big Tree as well as its 250-foot relatives.

The incense cedars have a reddish bark and sometimes are mistaken for Big Trees by the first-time visitors to the groves. You can avoid this trap by remembering that the bark of the Big Tree does not turn red until the tree matures and reaches a height of 200 or 250 feet and a girth of 8 or 10 feet. If you see a young, slender conifer with red bark, it's an incense cedar, not a Big Tree.

Because of the relative inaccessibility of many of the groves of Big Trees, you won't find as many motel-type accommodations and commercial developments as in the coast redwood belt. There are lodges in the national parks, however, and plenty of accommodations in the Central Valley towns that are within two or three hours' driving time of the groves.

Some of the groves are completely inaccessible during winter because of heavy snow. But the Generals' Highway between Sequoia and Kings Canyon parks is a road made to order for contemplation of the Western winter at its best and the Big Trees of the Sierra in an unusual setting. Except for brief closings during and after storms, the highway is kept open all winter. Between General Grant Grove and Giant Forest, you'll be able to drive leisurely and enjoy the cinnamon-red trunks of the Big Trees standing in warm contrast to the cool blue shadows and white highlights of the snow. A walk through snow-blanketed Giant Forest can be an enjoyable adventure.

GENERAL GRANT Tree, Kings Canyon National Park.

BIG STUMP, Calaveras Big Trees State Park.

YOUNG CLIMBERS *explore the massive roots of a fallen Big Tree in the Mariposa Grove of Yosemite National Park. About a dozen of the giants in the Mariposa Grove have fallen during historic times.*

The Central Sierra

Of the eight groves of Big Trees located north of the Kings River, only two are well known—the North Grove in Calaveras State Park and the Mariposa Grove in Yosemite National Park. All the others are accessible, but remote locations, lack of facilities, and limited numbers of large trees within groves tend to discourage most casual explorers. Experienced mountain drivers and hikers can have some fun seeking out the smaller groves in more remote locations, and summer crowds tend to be smaller in the national forests than in the national and state parks.

Placer County Grove

The northernmost grove of Big Trees is the Placer County or American River Grove, located in Tahoe National Forest about 40 miles northeast of Auburn. It is far from any other Big Trees (the closest are in Calaveras State Park, 50 miles to the south) and is one of the smallest of the named groves, with only six mature trees scattered over five acres.

The isolated location of the grove and its lack of natural reproduction make it somewhat of a curiosity. But because of the miles of twisting road that connect Placer County Grove with civilization, and the scarcity of mature giants at road's end, this area is not generally visited except by real buffs who are determined to see all of the Big Trees.

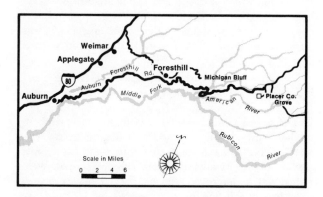

PLACER COUNTY GROVE is reached by unpaved road; check conditions before making off-season trips.

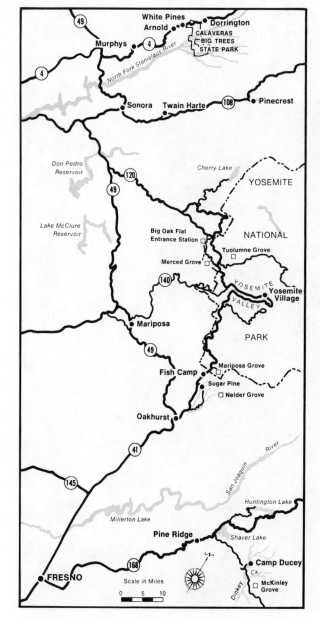

BIG TREE GROVES in the Central Sierra can easily be visited from nearby recreation areas.

DWARFED BY GIANTS, a lone visitor follows trail in North Grove of Calaveras-Big Trees State Park.

Calaveras-Big Trees State Park

This park includes two important groves of Big Trees—the well-developed and very popular North Grove, and the larger, more beautiful South Grove that was opened to visitors for the first time in 1969.

The North Grove contains about 100 mature trees and is a popular spot in both winter and summer. Families and organized groups flock to the park's campgrounds during the warm months, and there is enough snow in winter to attract a big crowd of snow bunnies who want to toboggan or build a snowman without fussing with lodges and ski runs.

You can explore the North Grove in about an hour by taking the self-guiding nature trail. Booklets available near the trail's start give details on the trees along the way. The most famous attraction is the Big Stump, which is the base of a giant tree that was first discovered in 1852 and was cut down in 1853. For decades after the cutting, the stump was used for dances and exhibits, and at one time, a pavilion was built to increase its all-year usage. It is said that 32 persons were able to dance on it at one time.

Big Stump's statistics provide a good example of how size and age of the Big Trees are not directly related. If this tree were standing today, it would be the largest of all the Big Trees, including those found in Sequoia and Kings Canyon National Parks. Estimates on its age would range from 2,500 years up to 4,000 years or more. But in fact, the tree was found to be only 1,320 years old when cut down. Great stature depends more on the supply of sunshine, water, and nutrients than on age.

The largest standing tree in the North Grove is the Empire State, 19 feet in diameter at chest level. It was probably surpassed at one time by the Mother of the Forest, which fell victim to one of the worst atrocities ever committed to any tree. This reportedly was a beautiful Big Tree, with a massive trunk and elegant branches. In 1854, all of the bark was stripped off the tree to a height of 116 feet and taken abroad to illustrate the size of the Sierra's Big Trees. The denuded tree was left to die, which it did, much to the anguish of everyone except the owners of the bark. Its naked trunk was one of the sorriest sights in the mountains, and it was almost a relief when a fire in 1910 reduced it to a charred snag.

Calaveras State Park's South Grove is the most beautiful collection of Big Trees in the central Sierra. It is only about six miles from the North Grove, but lack of access roads has kept it virtually inaccessible to all but hardy hikers, and even hardier motorists who were willing to navigate a circuitous route over forest service roads. Finally, in 1969, the two groves were linked with an improved road and the public was encouraged to visit this fine forest, where the red bark of more than 900 mature Big Trees brightens the dense stands of pine and fir.

TWO SNOWMEN take shape after a January snowfall at Calaveras-Big Trees State Park, a good place for very young children or for others not especially interested in skiing.

The discovery of the Calaveras Big Trees is one of the most popular anecdotes in the Sierra Nevada. In 1852 a hunter named A. T. Dowd accidentally stumbled across the trees while chasing a wounded bear. He excitedly returned to a mining camp near Murphys to report his find, but despite all his enthusiasm, no one would believe the descriptions—surely no tree could be that big. So skeptical were the miners that none would even accompany Dowd on a return trip into the mountains to verify his story.

Dowd bit his lip and waited a few days until everyone had forgotten about the trees. Then he again rushed into the camp and reported that he had killed the biggest grizzly bear he'd ever seen. Naturally, everyone rushed out to see the beast, and Dowd led them right into the heart of the redwoods. "Now, boys," Dowd reportedly said, "do you believe my tree story? That is the large grizzly I wanted you to see. Do you still think it a yarn?"

Swimming, fishing, boating. The Stanislaus River and its tributaries provide good fishing, and there are both wading shallows and deeper swimming pools. At one point the river drops sharply over a series of rocky ledges into a pool that is deep enough for diving. Granite ledges and smooth rocks make good sun-bathing spots. Expert boaters often take their kayaks and rubber rafts into the white-water canyon of the North Fork above Parrotts Ferry Bridge.

PIONEERS' CABIN has been burned, topped by a storm, tunneled by man—but it still grows.

WIDE ENOUGH *for most of today's cars, tunnel through Dead Giant was cut during stagecoach days.*

MOST PHOTOGRAPHED *of all Big Trees was Wawona Tree, until it toppled over in 1969.*

Yosemite National Park

There are three Big Tree groves in Yosemite, including the world-famous Mariposa Grove.

Northernmost of the three is the Tuolumne, located on the old Big Oak Flat Road that once served as the northern entrance to the park before State Route 120 was realigned and improved. The old road is one-way to the north, so motorists who visit the Tuolumne Grove must make a 17-mile loop trip.

There are 25 living mature Big Trees in the 60-acre grove. But the most famous tree has been dead for a long time. The Dead Giant already was a burned-out stump when first discovered, but enterprising publicists put it to good use by cutting a tunnel through the big trunk in 1878 and routing the stage road so travelers passed through the stump on their way to the park.

Most modern cars will still fit through the hole in the Dead Giant, but no trailers or pickup campers should make the attempt.

The Merced Grove is the least-visited grove of Big Trees in Yosemite. It includes only 20 of the trees, scattered over a fairly large area that is reached via a steep side road that branches off State Route 120. For a good part of the year, the lower one mile of this access road is hiking (all uphill on the way back).

The Mariposa Grove includes about 200 Big Trees, and even though no camping or picnicking is allowed, more than 400,000 visitors walk among the trees every year.

A tram system was recently introduced at Yosemite to relieve bumper-to-bumper traffic. Five trams carrying 50 persons each travel through the heart of the Mariposa Grove at the south edge of the park. No private vehicles are allowed within the grove.

The tram makes several stops along the roadway, enabling passengers to step off and wander around at their own pace, resuming the tour later. Park naturalists are on duty at two stops, the Grizzly Giants and the Mariposa Grove Museum.

Formerly, the big attraction at the Mariposa Grove was the Wawona Tree, more familiarly known as the "Drive-Through Tree." This tree had been photographed a million times by visitors who posed the family car inside the tunnel and grouped the family around the edges for the classic scrapbook shot.

The tunnel was cut in 1881 as a novelty to attract visitors to the area. Stagecoaches of the day had no trouble maneuvering through the nine-foot height and seven-foot width, nor did the thousands of automobiles that used to go through it. The cutting of the tunnel seems to have had little effect on the health of the Wawona Tree, even though its growth rate had slowed down since 1881. One winter morning in 1969 the tree was found toppled in

GALEN CLARK, GUARDIAN OF THE GRANT

It seems fitting that a man who grew up near mountains and forests should be the first to explore, name, and watch over the largest grove of Big Trees in Yosemite National Park. Galen Clark spent his early years enjoying the thick stands of spruces, birch, and maple in Massachusetts, and devoted his mature years to other peoples' enjoyment of the Big Tree forests of the Sierra.

Clark was born in Canada in 1814, and seemed destined to a quiet life as a furniture maker in Massachusetts. But his weak lungs could not tolerate the continuous exposure to wood dust. When his wife died of consumption in 1848, Galen left his five children with relatives and set out for California to seek wealth and health. After an unsuccessful try at mining, he went to work for John C. Fremont in Mariposa. But three years after his arrival, Galen suffered a severe lung hemorrhage and a local physician suggested that a move to a mountain climate might prolong his life. Galen recalled some warm days he had spent in Yosemite the previous summer while camping with a survey party, and set out immediately to establish his new home in the higher climes.

In March, 1856, Galen pitched his tent across the meadow from the present-day Wawona Hotel and claimed 160 acres of the meadow. Bearded, shaggy-haired, often going barefoot and hatless to aid his circulation, Galen spent his first months hunting, fishing, befriending the Indians, and familiarizing himself with the Yosemite environs.

During his explorations Galen watched constantly for some red-barked trees that he had heard about from members of the survey party. He hoped to use them as an attraction to encourage more people to travel the Mariposa trail and visit Yosemite. In June, 1857, while exploring the area a few miles north of his campsite, Galen finally came across the giant trees. These Big Trees had first been discovered in 1849 by Major Burney, who later became sheriff of Mariposa. But Burney thought they were cedars and he told few people about them for fear of being ridiculed for exaggerating about their size. Clark explored the grove thoroughly and named it Mariposa Grove of Big Trees after the county in which they were growing.

Galen welcomed visitors to Clark's Station, as his campsite came to be called, and guided them to the giant trees and to Yosemite Valley. John and Jessie Fremont, Ralph Waldo Emerson, and John Muir were among his guests. He guided photographers and often posed for pictures in front of the Grizzly Giant — a rugged looking man in front of a rugged looking tree. Early in 1864 Clark built an emergency shelter in the middle of the Mariposa Grove. The present museum stands on that site.

Galen gained a reputation for providing delicious meals of roasted squirrel, deer liver, trout, homemade bread, and strawberry jam. He did most of his own cooking but had some Indian help.

BIG TREES shade Galen Clark's Yosemite grave.

In June, 1864, President Lincoln signed a bill granting Yosemite Valley and the Mariposa Grove to the state of California and the Governor was instructed by Congress to appoint an eight-man Board of Commissioners to manage the grant. Galen was named to the Board and two years later was appointed first Guardian of the Grant.

For fifteen years Galen watched over the trees, plants, and wildlife of the area, helped campers keep their food from bears, and answered numerous questions about the trees. Then political developments brought about the appointment of a new Board of Commissioners, and James Hutchings replaced Clark as Guardian. Galen remained in the Valley area, operating a truck farm and driving his buggy for tourists who wished to hire him. He also spent some time preparing the gravesite he had chosen in the Yosemite cemetery. He planted some Big Trees and watered them from a well dug for that purpose.

In June, 1889, at the age of 75, Clark was again appointed Guardian. He succeeded James McCord, a political appointee whose inexperience and limited knowledge of Yosemite had caused him to be fired. Galen attended to his routine duties and was often seen conducting rugged hiking tours for interested persons. Yosemite National Park was created in 1890, and Galen retired as Guardian of the Grant six years later.

On March 24, 1910, 54 years after his arrival in Yosemite, Galen Clark died. He had indeed found health in the mountain climate, and had devoted nearly a lifetime to preserving the beauty that had given him a new lease on life.

THE GRIZZLY GIANT is fifth largest of Sierra Big Trees. Lightning storms have flattened its crown.

MARIPOSA GROVE MUSEUM is open summer months. A visit will help you learn about the trees.

the snow. No one knows exactly what killed the tree, but the heavy foot traffic around the tree had eroded several inches of the soil around the base and could have weakened it enough to make it fall.

The most startling tree in appearance in the Mariposa Grove is the Grizzly Giant—not the tallest or the thickest of the Big Trees, but certainly the one with the most character. This old monster has been through storms, fires, lightning, drought, and flood—and shows it. The limbs are twisted and broken, the crown is flattened, the trunk is scarred in a dozen places, and the whole tree tilts precariously as if it were about to fall over from exhaustion.

But looks are deceiving. The Grizzly Giant is a healthy tree. In fact, there are indications that it is the fastest growing Big Tree in the Mariposa Grove. The latest estimates place its age at about 2,700 years (perhaps the oldest of all the Big Trees), and it still grows faster than trees half its age. The rapid growth is probably due to favorable underground drainage that provides a constant source of moisture through most of the year.

Near the Grizzly Giant is the California Tree, which was tunneled in 1895. At one time, stagecoaches were allowed to pass through its trunk when the winter snows prevented them from reaching the Wawona Tree. In 1932, the roads were realigned and the California Tree was permanently set aside for pedestrian sightseers only.

There are many fallen trees in Mariposa Grove. About six of these have toppled since 1916 when the National Park Service began administering the area. One of the oldest and most famous of the down trees is the Fallen Monarch, along the main road near the entrance to the grove. It has been lying there for as long as anyone can remember, and the heartwood is still in good condition.

A fascinating example of the ability of the Big Trees to withstand fire is the Corridor Tree, across the road from the Fallen Monarch. This living tree has been so badly eaten away by fire that the main trunk is attached to the roots by only six shafts of sapwood.

Nelder Grove

Nelder Grove is just a few miles south of the southern entrance to Yosemite National Park. It is reached via a winding, dirt road from State Route 41, and may be impossible to reach at all during wet weather. The area has been extensively logged, and its rough appearance is a far cry from the paved roads and combed trails of the Mariposa Grove.

The grove is named for John A. Nelder, a hermit who lived in the area in the 1870's. John Muir came across him while exploring the Big Trees, and wrote:

"While wandering about surveying the boundaries of the grove, anxious to see every tree, I came suddenly on a handsome log cabin, richly embowered and so fresh and unweathered it was still redolent of gum and balsam like a newly felled tree. Strolling forward, wondering who could have built it, I found an old, weary-eyed, speculative, gray-haired man on a bark stool by the door, reading a book. . . he bade me welcome, made me bring my mule down to a little slanting meadow before his door and camp with him, promising to show me his pet trees and many curious things bearing on my studies.

". . . since '49 he had wandered over most of the Sierra, sinking innumerable prospect holes like a sailor making soundings, digging new channels for streams, sifting gold-sprinkled boulder and gravel beds with unquenchable energy, life's noon the meanwhile passing unnoticed into late afternoon shadows. Then, health and gold gone, the game played and lost, like a wounded deer creeping into this forest solitude, he awaits the sundown call. . . The name of my hermit friend is John A. Nelder, a fine kind man, who in going into the woods has at last gone home; for he loves nature truly, and realizes that these last shadowy days with scarce a glint of gold in them are the best of all."

Most of Nelder Grove's biggest trees were logged before 1900, and less than 50 of the real giants are left —ignored by the woodcutters because of their unwieldy size or impractical locations. The grove is dotted with high stumps that indicate the size of the lost trees.

Only two of the trees are labeled. The Bull Buck Tree is a handsome specimen that appears even more grand next to the ugly stumps that stand nearby. The Sierra Beauty is along the dirt road that enters the grove from Sugar Pine. Close by the Sierra Beauty is a small campground and a self-guiding nature trail.

Since the logging operations stopped, there has been a great surge of natural reproduction within the grove. You'll find many stands of uniformly-sized trees, ranging in age from 10 to 50 years.

McKinley Grove

This is a fine grove of Big Trees that is seldom visited because of its remote location and lack of facilities. There is a small picnic area and scenic overlook immediately north of the grove, and a parking area and rest rooms near the entrance, but no campgrounds, ranger stations, or self-guiding nature trails. The grove is choked with fallen wood and thick undergrowth that discourages hiking.

The walk into the main part of the grove is steep and there are no trails to follow. If you stay close to the creek and take your time, you can make your way gradually up into the higher slopes where there are dozens of handsome Big Trees. For a narrow loop trip, walk uphill on the north side of the ravine, cross over when you get tired, and walk back through the trees on the south side. This is most pleasant in May and June when the dogwood is flowering and the stream is running full. To explore the area further, follow the creek bed down to the brink of the Dinkey Creek Canyon.

VISITORS to Big Tree groves are encouraged to stay on paths to avoid damaging trees' root systems.

HIGH STUMPS in Nelder Grove are reminders of wasteful logging practices of early 20th century.

A SNOWY FOREST *awaits the winter visitor to Sequoia National Park. Much of the park is closed, but you can explore the Giant Forest on foot. Accommodations are available; ski area is just four miles away.*

Sequoia and Kings Canyon National Parks

It is in the groves in these two national parks that the Big Trees of the Sierra reach their highest attainment, both in the overall number of trees and individual development. Here is the tallest Big Tree, the thickest, and the greatest in total bulk. The closest thing to a pure stand of these trees is in the Sugar Bowl area of Redwood Mountain Grove, and what many people consider to be the finest stand in the world—the Congress Group—is on a well-worn trail in the Giant Forest.

This is also the area of greatest study on the Big Trees. Their age, growth patterns, and reproduction are under constant scrutiny in Sequoia and Kings Canyon National Parks and in Whitaker's Forest, and detailed studies have been conducted on the effects of human traffic on the groves. Results of these experiments are now beginning to provide the data that is needed to encourage longevity of the virgin trees and abundant natural reproduction.

Big Stump Basin

This 800-acre basin just north of the Highway 180 entrance into Kings Canyon National Park was heavily logged in the 1880's. Virtually all of the Big Trees were cut for the mills, so that today there are only a few virgin trees on the fringes of a stump-ridden area of small, second-growth trees.

In this basin you will see the Sawed Tree, which is gradually healing a wound caused by loggers in the 1880's, the Mark Twain Stump, and Old Adam or Burnt Monarch. The Mark Twain was one of the largest trees in the world when it was cut in 1891 to become an exhibit in the American Museum of Natural History in New York. The stump is still 24 feet across, and was probably larger when it was freshly cut and still had its sapwood and bark. Despite its size, the tree was less than 1,500 years old when cut. Burnt Monarch is a huge, burned out, hollow stump of a former Big Tree that was known as Old Adam. Some historians believe that Old Adam was the biggest of all the Big Trees—but there is no way of proving or disproving any of the claims made about trees cut down before the days of precise measurement.

The self-guiding Big Stump Trail starts at the parking area less than a mile from the entrance station. You can pick up a descriptive leaflet from dispenser boxes at the start of the trail.

BIG TREES reach their peak in numbers, size, and beauty in and around the national parks.

General Grant Grove

This is the logical destination of all visitors to Kings Canyon National Park—it is the largest grove of Big Trees in the park, and it is close to the main park facilities. The road into the Grant Grove takes you almost to the base of the General Grant Tree, to its towering companions (many named for states) and to the Dead Giant and Fallen Monarch. The area is easily explored, and paved trails wind among the most popular Big Trees.

The General Grant is believed to be the second largest tree in the world. It is some 267 feet high, and more than 40 feet in diameter at the base. It is a handsome tree and a great favorite of photographers, who have a rare opportunity to back away from the giant and get its full height dramatically in view. The General Grant is known as The Nation's Christmas Tree, and each December it is the scene of special religious and patriotic services. The first of these services was held in 1925, and the tree was designated as a national shrine by congressional action in 1956.

Horses were once sheltered in the strong, hollow shell of the Fallen Monarch, and the pioneer Gamlin Brothers used it for a temporary home in 1871 while they built a cabin, which still stands within the Grant Grove.

The Centennial Stump is the base of a giant that was cut in 1875 to provide an exhibit for the Philadelphia Exposition of 1876. A 16-foot section of the outer shell was exhibited, but Easterners were reluctant to believe that any tree could grow to that size.

LIGHTNING TREE is one of several named giants in the small but very popular General Grant Grove.

TWENTY-THREE STANDEES aren't even crowded atop 24-foot-wide Mark Twain Stump.

SAWED TREE was partly cut by loggers in 1880's, but it didn't fall and is gradually covering wound.

UNDERCUT is made in Big Tree. Photograph was taken in Mountain Home area about 1904.

SLICE is cut from downed tree by workers who were prisoners in local jails (note covered faces).

CUTTING THE BIG TREES WAS A BIG JOB

Forget for a moment the wastefulness and shortsightedness of the lumber companies that cut down the Big Trees and consider the problems involved in cutting down one of these giants. How did the early lumbermen do it? Without the benefit of power saws and modern know-how, they had to rely on physical strength and endurance—and some explosives—to fell trees that were 250 feet or more high and 25 feet thick. It was the toughest lumbering job imaginable, and the feats of the men who did the cutting make up some of California's favorite folklore.

The huge buttresses of the mature Big Trees were considered unmanageable by the early lumbermen. They built platforms—often supported by "spokes" imbedded in the tree trunks—and started cutting 10 to 20 feet off the ground. The height of the first cut was lowered considerably as the men became more experienced, but even then, it was the rare Big Tree that was sliced off at ground level.

Once the height of the cut was established, two men with axes would chop a deep, high notch in one side of the tree. This was the undercut and had to be carefully carved out to guarantee an accurate fall. The men sometimes worked for days on a single undercut, which had to be as much as eight feet tall and twelve feet deep. Some of the woodcutters added unnecessary height to the notch, so they could pose for photos while standing or sitting on a horse inside the cut.

When the undercut was completed, two men attacked the tree on the opposite side, this time with a long cross-cut saw that was pulled back and forth by the hour. Steel wedges were driven into the cut to keep the tree from settling back and binding the saw.

The sawing was continued until the teeth were within a few inches of the undercut. At this point—after six or seven days of back-breaking work—the tree was ready to fall. The saw was removed and more wedges were driven into the cut to force the tree off balance toward the undercut. Once tipped, there was no stopping or slowing the fall, and the tree came down with earthquake force.

The brittle character of the wood of the Big Trees made the cutting a very wasteful process. When a heavy tree hit the ground, it usually shattered into hundreds of pieces, many of which were totally useless as lumber. Damage was the worst when the ground was uneven. The lumbermen tried to solve this problem by preparing a bed for the tree—a cushion of small branches, leaves, and bark to break the force of the fall. This required many extra man hours of work, but wood recovery definitely was improved.

Downed trees that were too large to fit on the railcars or to be moved any other way had to be broken into smaller pieces with blasting powder. The blasters always tried to make the wood split lengthwise, but more often than not, the blasting only served to fracture the trees into uneven chunks that were impractical for the mill.

The lumbermen could see all of this terrible waste as they cut the Big Trees, but it did not deter their efforts. Even after leaving most of the wood on the forest floor, they were still able to cut more boards and shingles and stakes out of a single Big Tree than they could from any other tree—and the dream of quick riches was overbearing, even though it was never fulfilled.

IN A QUIET MEADOW, visitors to the Giant Forest walk among young Big Trees. The trees will retain their conical shape until they are 75 to 100 years old. Natural reproduction in southern range is good.

IMPRESSIVE STATISTICS of General Grant and General Sherman trees are displayed in Grant Grove.

Just beyond the Grant Grove parking lot is a one-way dirt road that loops through the North Grove of Big Trees. Very few visitors ever bother making the trip, so when Grant Grove is crowded you can drive a mile west and enjoy an undisturbed forest of Big Trees.

Grant Grove Village

A mile from the General Grant Tree, beside a big meadow, is Grant Grove Village. This is the activity center for Kings Canyon National Park, with a store, service station, post office, ranger station, lodge, coffee shop, dining room, cocktail lounge, and gift shop. Ranger-naturalists conduct daily one and two-hour nature walks, and illustrated talks are given at campfire programs held every night in summer.

Converse Basin

The logging history of Converse Basin is enough to make strong men retch. In this four-mile-long basin once

THE MIDDLE FORK of the Kings River tumbles through a rocky gorge on its way from high country.

PATRIARCH of the trees in General Grant Grove is General Grant Tree, second largest of all Big Trees.

stood the most beautiful of all the forests of Big Trees. Thousands of mature Big Trees were mixed in a thick forest of fir and pine, and some of the giants probably were larger than the General Sherman and General Grant trees, now recognized as the largest living trees.

Between 1897 and 1907, this entire basin was wiped out. Something like 8,000 trees were cut by lumbermen who could not pass up this tremendous source of wood, even though the lumber was of limited value. Many of the tree trunks were never used because they shattered when they hit the ground or were too big and costly to move. The logging operation never made a nickel for any of the lumber companies, but it destroyed an incalculable natural fortune.

The basin is named after Charles P. Converse, one of the first to think of logging the area. He was able to get financial backing, but a recession in 1876 killed the whole idea. Later attempts by more established companies succeeded, however, and in 1897 about 400 men began to cut down the trees. Every summer for 10

years, the men came and cut the trees. There were accidents, high expenses, breakdowns in the machinery—but still the cutters continued until there was little left.

They cut down most of the mature trees. One that was left was The Boole Tree, which was found in 1903 at the northern end of the basin. It was one of the largest in the area, and for some reason was never cut. It may have been that it was too big to be cut and moved profitably. Perhaps the Forest Service intervened. At any rate, it was left standing and was named after Frank Boole, who managed the logging operation for most of the 10 years. The tree is 269 feet high and 35 feet in diameter at the base—one of the largest of all the Big Trees.

The present road down into Converse Basin is rough and steep, and is usually reserved for four-wheel-drive vehicles. If you are determined to explore the area, ask the rangers on duty at the Grant Grove Village Visitor Center whether the road is improved enough for your particular vehicle.

CHARRED STUMP is all that remains of General Noble Tree, which may have been largest of all Big Trees.

HUME LAKE was once the site of a lumber mill. Today it is enjoyed as a fishing and boating area.

Chicago Stump

Converse Basin was not the only area of Big Trees that was disastrously logged. Between 1862 and 1900, lumbering companies denuded many of the best forests south of the canyon of the Kings River. Just south of Converse Basin are the remains of just such a forest, now known as the Chicago Stump area.

When it was still standing, the Chicago Stump was known as the General Noble Tree, and some old-timers believe that it was bigger than the General Sherman. It was cut in 1893 to be taken to the Chicago World's Exposition. The first cut was made 50 feet off the ground. The tall stump was then hollowed out, cut into pieces and taken to Chicago, where it was reassembled, roofed over, and opened for inspection. However, visitors thought that the exhibit must have been made up from the parts of several trees, and the display was called the California Hoax.

To reach the Chicago Stump, you drive two miles through an area that was heavily logged and then repeatedly burned. Some of the stumps have been reduced to cinders, and all of them—including the Chicago Stump —show the effects of repeated fires. Post-fire Big Tree seedlings are growing by the hundreds. Some still have the conical shape of youth, and others are beginning to assume their mature form.

Indian Basin Grove

This is another grove that was once known for its exceptional beauty, but was completely and devastatingly logged in the late nineteenth century. The original forest straddled the present Highway 180 between the intersections with Hume Lake Road and the Converse Mountain Loop Road. You can walk through the area and see the remains of the skid roads that were used to move the fallen trees. The abundance and size of the Big Tree stumps attest to the grandeur of the original grove, which reputedly was a favorite trading grounds for the Indians. There are no giant trees here, but you will see a small group of specimens with 10-foot diameters, and several patches of healthy second growth.

Hume Lake Area

This region is not actually within the confines of Kings Canyon National Park, but is on Sequoia National Forest lands between the General Grant and Cedar Grove areas of the national park.

There are about a dozen Big Tree groves in the mountains south and east of Hume Lake. Some along the forks of Boulder Creek are accessible only by trail, and a couple of others require some tough dirt-road driving. The best way to see a selection of the trees in this area is via the new road that starts at Hume Lake and leads east to Evans Grove, the largest and most attractive stand in this area. There are about 500 mature trees in Evans Grove, most within easy walking distance.

Along this road you'll pass near the Lockwood and Horseshoe Bend groves. The Lockwood Grove contains about 25 mature trees and makes a pleasant stopping point between Hume Lake and Evans Grove.

The Hume Lake area was the scene of some extensive logging operations after 1910. There was a mill on the northern end of the lake, and a locomotive hauled the trees from forest to mill until about 1917.

Gateway to the High Country

A 30-mile, non-park road from Grant Grove takes you to Cedar Grove, starting point for trips into the park's back country. The drive is a beautiful one along the South Fork of the Kings River. There is a long-term parking area at the end of the road where you can leave your car while you take off on trips into the depths of the park. This is a favorite gateway to the high country, and from road's end you can watch the stream of hikers, backpackers, and pack trains heading into the mountains. If you do not have the time or inclination to take an extended trip into the back country, there are a number of short, easy hikes you can take in the Cedar Grove area.

Redwood Mountain Grove

Redwood Mountain and Redwood Canyon—a trough that runs parallel to the mountain in its afternoon shade —are lumped together as the Redwood Mountain Grove. This 4,500-acre forest ranks as the largest of the Big Tree groves, and many authorities consider it to be the most beautiful.

The huge valley and mountain ridge of Big Trees is off the beaten track and many people miss it. The lack of crowds adds to its charm. On the canyon floor or on the slopes of the mountain you can walk for minutes at a time through nearly pure stands of Big Trees. In density of the dominant species, this area is like some of the larger coast redwood groves.

The Big Trees reach their peak in the Sugar Bowl, which is as close to a pure stand of Big Trees as you will find anywhere. At one spot, you can count 57 lofty giants within view (see page 77). The grove has the cathedral quality of several other more famous groves of Big Trees and coast redwoods, but without the constant flow of people (it is 2½ miles from Sugar Bowl to the nearest automobile road).

Sugar Bowl and Barton's Post Camp—both destinations for guided tours that are conducted from Grant Grove Village in the summer months—can be reached on comparatively short walks (5 miles and 2½ miles round trip, respectively). But the best way to see the Redwood Mountain Grove is to continue past these points on an all-day loop of about eight miles through more Big Trees and patches of manzanita, alongside pretty streams with waterfalls, to the Hart Tree (fourth largest of the Big Trees), and back to the starting point.

AWE-INSPIRING giants line the trail to Barton's Post Camp, a quiet grove in Redwood Canyon.

A LONG-DISTANCE VIEW of Big Trees on Redwood Mountain can be enjoyed from Generals' Highway.

A YOUNG SPRINTER dashes along the broad trunk of a fallen Big Tree in Redwood Canyon.

A WALK THROUGH a hollow Big Tree log is part of conducted trip to Sugar Bowl on Redwood Mountain.

The best starting place for all walks in Redwood Mountain Grove is a parking lot at the site of a former CCC camp at the foot of a 1.7-mile dirt road that drops down into the canyon from Generals' Highway, about five miles south of Grant Grove Village.

Redwood Mountain Overlook is a viewpoint on the Generals' Highway. From it you can look down into the canyon and out along the spine of Redwood Mountain. It's a good place to get a general lay of the land, and anyone who's going to make the eight-mile loop would do well to stop here for a general survey before starting off on foot.

Whitaker's Forest

Whitaker's Forest is a 320-acre piece of the Redwood Mountain Grove that is administered by the University of California. It was given to the University in 1910 by Horace Whitaker (see page 78), and has been used for forestry studies since 1915.

Currently, it is the scene of important studies on the ecology of the Big Trees. More than 60 acres of the Forest have been "manipulated" to determine ways to protect the present stands of Big Trees and to encourage future growth.

The idea of manipulation and forest management are not new in the Big Tree groves. When the first conservationists and forest officials instituted the first fire prevention programs, they began to "manage" the forests. Fire prevention programs were badly needed to preserve the Big Trees, develop recreational facilities, and encourage timber forests. But a curious thing has happened. By protecting the groves, the authorities have created a totally unnatural situation that is seriously impairing the reproduction of the Big Trees and placing them in their greatest danger from fire.

The unnatural situation that has resulted from the suppression of fire was aptly described in the 1963 report of the special advisory board on wildlife management to Secretary of the Interior Stewart Udall. In part the report stated:

"When the forty-niners poured over the Sierra Nevada into California, those that kept diaries spoke almost to a man of the wide-spaced columns of mature trees that grew on the western slope in gigantic magnificence. The ground was a grass parkland, in springtime carpeted with wildflowers. Deer and bear were abundant.

"Today, much of the west slope is a dog-hair thicket of young pines, white fir, incense-cedar, and mature brush—a direct function of over protection from natural ground fires. Within the national parks . . . the thickets are even more impenetrable than elsewhere. Not only is this accumulation of fuel dangerous to the giant sequoias and other mature trees, but the animal life is meager, wildflowers are sparse, and to some at least the vegetation is depressing, not uplifting.

"Is it possible that the primitive open forest could be restored, at least on a local scale? And, if so, how?"

PUREST OF ALL stands of Big Trees is Sugar Bowl. From one point you can see 57 of the red-barked giants.

THE LONELY WORLD OF HORACE WHITAKER

Horace Whitaker, the man who gave his forest to the University of California, was one of the Sierra's most eccentric pioneers and conservationists. He was a tall, lean farmer with a flowing beard, a passion for argument, and an intense dislike of firearms, dogs, and women. He led the life of a recluse, and explained the foibles of other folk with a favorite expression, "It's a queer world we live in."

According to Orlena Barton Wrought—one of Whitaker's long-time neighbors and his unofficial biographer—young Horace came to California from Connecticut in 1856. He settled down in Tulare County in 1858 on a ranch located a few miles from the present town of Orosi. Two of Whitaker's traits quickly became apparent to other settlers. One, he was an excellent farmer, and knew how to invest his earnings in promising parcels of land. Two, he was a cranky old devil. Horace didn't like neighbors and would kick up a fuss every time a new house went up within miles of his own. He put up gates across public roads to keep the settlers out of the foothills, and then argued his case for privacy both in and out of court.

Whitaker evidently had a streak of kleptomania in his personality and this, along with his argumentative nature, did not encourage invitations to the local bridge club. He did not welcome visitors to his own ranch, and kept pet skunks around the house allegedly to catch mice but also to discourage nosy neighbors. He needed hired hands to help with the work, but his miserliness kept them in short supply.

Whitaker may not have been very fond of people, but he loved the land. And the tract that he loved the most was a 320-acre parcel of Redwood Mountain that he bought in 1900. The area had been logged in the 1870's but still had some virgin Big Trees, and good second growths of Big Trees, pine, and fir. He built a little cabin and spent many summer days enjoying the solitude of the remote location.

When Whitaker's health began to fail in the early part of the twentieth century, he decided to do something about preserving his favorite Sierra retreat. After conferring with Benjamin Ide Wheeler, President of the University of California, Whitaker deeded the forest to the university in 1910, with the provisions that the land be used for forestry instruction and public recreation.

Just two months later, Whitaker was dead at age 80. Characteristically, he cut off his relatives without a cent and left his estate to the descendants of a few old friends. But the relatives were able to break the will, sell his ranch properties, and divide the returns. They also tried to recover the land that had been deeded to the university, but without success.

Whitaker was buried in an unmarked grave near his ranch for about 25 years. The university and local historical groups finally had the casket unearthed and moved to Whitaker's Forest where it now lies under a grove of young Big Trees.

Whitaker's simple habits are best expressed in his oft-repeated recipe for cooking vegetables. "Put the kettle of water on to boil, let it boil like hell, then drop the cleaned vegetables in, keep them boiling that same way. When done let each fellow season to his own taste." Whitaker seasoned life to his own taste, and if some others didn't like it—well, it's a queer world we live in.

The authorities' basic mistake was believing that all fires, including those originating from natural causes, were bad. Fire prevention meant *total* fire prevention, so that most of the Big Trees that are protected in national parks and forests have not been through a fire of any kind for at least seventy or eighty years.

In contrast, fire was a common visitor to the Sierra before 1850. Virtually every mature Big Tree has at least one fire scar, and many have been seriously burned a dozen times or more. Frequent surface fires were started by lightning, and these fires consumed the debris and destroyed some young trees that grew up around the mature giants. It has been estimated that the "unmanaged" forest can expect to be visited by fire at least every eight years—and one detailed study showed that a portion of Stanislaus National Forest was burned 221 times between 1454 and 1912—an average of one fire every two years. Dozens of lightning fires start in the Sierra every year, which probably means that fire was actually an annual occurrence in some part of the forest before men started fire prevention programs. Repeated burning kept the forest open and clear, and major fires were rare.

It is true that fires destroyed thousands of young trees that had not yet developed thick bark and foliage-free trunks, but the fires also helped natural reforestation. The seeds of the Big Trees cannot get started unless they are implanted in mineral soil (see page 12), and fires served to burn away the duff and needles covering this soil. Once a fire had burned off the available fuel in a grove, that area would remain free of fire for some time and seedlings had a better chance to survive.

Experiments in Whitaker's Forest cover several aspects of forest management:

1. The amount of fuel—down wood, young growing trees, brush—is being substantially reduced. After this area was logged of pines and Big Trees in the 1870's, heavy stands of second-growth Big Trees, incense cedar, white fir, and willow quickly grew in the open areas. This young growth has grown unchecked during the fire-prevention years until it now presents a very dangerous situation. On Redwood Mountain, the fuel has increased to such a level that any small fire might quickly develop into an uncontrollable conflagration with the strength to destroy the entire grove. The Whitaker's Forest experimental plots are being cleared both by human effort and by small surface fires that consume fallen branches, pine needles, and debris.

2. Competitive trees are being removed. Young incense cedars, white fir, and other trees compete with the Big Trees for water and nutrients, so the growth pattern of the giants slows appreciably. If the competition is kept down—naturally by fire or unnaturally by chain saws and prescribed burning—the Big Trees get bigger faster. There are more than 200 old-growth Big Trees in Whitaker's, plus hundreds of young ones that undoubtedly will enter a faster growth cycle as they are supplied with a greater share of the available nutrients.

3. Scenic values are increasing. With young trees and brush cleared away, the aesthetic values of the groves definitely improve. Visitors can locate the trees at a greater distance, and appreciate their immense size.

4. Wildlife is encouraged. A forest that is choked with young trees and thick brush is a biological desert for mammals. They need browse, grasses, and young growth to survive. Deer, bear, and smaller mammals abandon the overgrown areas in favor of those that have been burned and cleared to allow new young shoots to appear.

5. Park-like conditions are being encouraged. To revive the open "natural" conditions in the groves, some trees (Big Trees, sugar pine) are being encouraged, and others (incense cedar, white fir) are being cut out almost entirely.

The current research project in Whitaker's Forest started in 1964 and will continue until 1972. The results achieved here could have a profound effect on forest practices both within the national parks and in the national forests where the dangers of serious fire increases with each passing year. Many conservationists and foresters reject the idea of prescribed burning within the forests, because they are aware of what can happen when a controlled fire becomes uncontrolled. Cutting young trees, cleaning up debris, and burning the slash is also a very expensive proposition—one estimate is $115-$150 an acre. But despite the costs, it now appears certain that something must be done to reduce the chance of disaster within the Big Tree groves, and it may well be that small-scale "friendly" fires are the best preventive maintenance against holocaust.

MANAGED GROVE in Whitaker's Forest was cleaned of debris to cut fire danger, encourage trees' growth.

UNMANAGED AREAS of Whitaker's Forest are choked with fallen wood, low growth. Fire danger is serious.

LOST GROVE is one of the smallest of the named groves in Sequoia National Park. Most of its trees are visible from the Generals' Highway, which cuts through the center of the grove.

GIANT PEAKS of the Great Western Divide stand out against the sky ahead of hiker on Alta Peak trail.

Lost Grove

Lost Grove is easy to find. The Generals' Highway cuts right through the center of it, and most of the mature Big Trees are within sight of the roadway. A walkway leads uphill to the largest of the trees.

This is one of several good spots within the park to see deer.

Muir Grove

Muir Grove is one of the largest and most appealing of the Big Tree groves in Sequoia National Park. Because it is reached only by a five-mile round trip hike, many visitors to the park don't bother to seek it out. It is not a difficult hike, however, and the rangers lead guided tours into the area every summer.

The trail starts at the far end of Dorst Campground and stays on the slopes south of Dorst Creek with a minimum of ups and downs. The steepest part of the trail is within the grove itself, and you can take it easy and enjoy the towering trees.

It is estimated that there are more than 1,500 trees in Muir Grove, several of which rank high on the list of "biggest" and "tallest." Many of the trees are arranged in tight clusters, and it is this density that gives the

THE SILENCE *of the wintery scene is broken only by the rumble of a rotary snowplow moving slowly along the Generals' Highway. Except for brief closings after heavy storms, the road is kept open all winter.*

grove much of its beauty and distinctiveness. The grove covers about 300 acres, so you can extend your exploration just as far as your legs allow.

The guided tours take five hours and hikers are asked to bring their lunches. You can do it faster on your own, if time is limited.

Giant Forest

This is the place. When most people think of the Big Trees, they think of the Giant Forest, where you can drive, hike, eat, sleep, shop, feed deer, and just sit in the shade of some of the most beautiful trees on earth.

Most of the park's tourist facilities are located in this area. The Giant Forest Museum is the information center for both parks. If you have time, visit the museum before you begin your explorations—there are large relief maps of the area and displays that explain the Big Trees, and park's geologic history, and the plant life you will see along the trails and roads.

The name Giant Forest—attributed to John Muir, who visited the area in 1875—applies to 2,387 acres of rolling benchland between the Marble and Middle forks of the Kaweah River. Deep river canyons isolate it on three sides; to the northeast, the ridge (of which it is a flattened part) sharpens and rises to timberline on

ACTIVITY CENTER *for Sequoia National Park is Giant Forest Village, with lodge, museum, store, post office.*

IT'S EASY WALKING among stately Big Trees in Giant Forest. Here young trees crowd into Causeway Meadow.

Alta Peak and continues northeastward, glaciated and bare, to a junction with the high divide between the Kaweah and Kings watersheds.

You can drive through the Giant Forest, craning to see the treetops, but you will miss the unforgettable experience that comes with a few hours of easy walking through the heart of this greatest surviving forest of Big Trees. The Congress Trail is an excellent place to start; it covers about one-third of the entire forest and takes you to the best concentration of wonders east of the Generals' Highway.

Congress Trail starts from the parking lot next to the General Sherman Tree, and you can spend a few minutes studying this largest of all trees before you start your walk. Don't expect the Sherman to stand out grandly from its neighbors, since there are half a dozen trees here—particularly the Lincoln, President, and McKinley—that are close to it in size. But still, it is an awesome sight, especially when you stand back and compare the size of its trunk and limbs to the ant-like humans who crowd around its base.

The Congress Trail covers an easy two miles and has been improved as a self-guiding nature route. Brochures are available from a box at the start of the walk.

Along the Congress Trail, you can see examples of virtually every important feature of the Big Trees. There are young conical trees, and very old trees, some symmetrical and others burned and gnarled into strange shapes. One tree is being undercut by a stream, and another has already fallen because of such undermining. Several have been burned by fire, and one is completely hollowed.

The high point of your walk is bound to be the House and Senate groups, which are to the Big Trees what the Rockefeller Grove is to the coast redwoods. These are massive, handsome trees soaring upward like so many giants standing guard over the lesser creatures of the world.

After this introduction to the Giant Forest, you may want to take off on your own with nothing more than the National Park Service trail map in your hand. You can stride vigorously through the woods, or take all day to cover a couple of miles. If you have one or two days to devote to leisurely contemplation, here are snail-paced itineraries that you may enjoy:

First day: Take Congress Trail to the Senate Group. Go left through the group and around the east side of Circle Meadow. Stop for lunch on a rocky knoll to the right of the trail, just beyond the meadow. Then continue past more meadows to Black Arch and Pillars of Hercules. Go past Cattle Cabin and through Founders' Group to Congress Trail and Sherman Tree. This round trip is about three miles.

Second day: Start on the short dirt spur road on the east side of the Generals' Highway, one-tenth mile south of the entrance to Pinewood Camp. Turn left on Rimrock Trail. Spend some time at the Cloister (four exceptionally fine trees) and have lunch at the foot of

MONKEY FLOWER *is one of over 1,200 kinds of plants that have been identified in these two parks.*

AT PARADISE CAMPGROUND *in Giant Forest area, you can set up camp in the shadow of giant trees.*

GENERAL SHERMAN TREE *is generally acknowledged to be the world's largest living thing.*

CRESCENT MEADOW, surrounded by forest, was described by John Muir as fairest portion of all Sierra.

IT'S EASY to climb Moro Rock, although it looks difficult. View from the top is spectacular.

A SNUG HOME was fashioned by Hale Tharp in this hollow log reached by trail from Crescent Meadow.

Lincoln Tree, or if it's too early, go on down Alta Trail to the southwest, turn left to Bear's Bathtub and Black Causeway and stop there. Follow around to the right, past Shattered Giant and Washington Tree, and back to Alta Trail. Just past the Indian mortars, keep right for the Generals' Highway. This is another three-mile loop.

The Crescent Meadow Road from Giant Forest Village leads through more of the Giant Forest area and takes motorists to several unusual single trees and groupings. The Auto Log is a fallen tree that has been leveled on top so that you can drive your car right onto the trunk. You can't drive very far, but it makes a great picture for the folks back home.

Triple Tree is the name applied to three large trees that are growing from a single base. The Parker Group, one of the finest small groups in this area, is named after a U.S. Cavalry officer. The Tunnel Log is a Big Tree that fell across the road in 1937 and was cut to permit the passage of vehicles. The cut is only eight feet high, however, so pickup campers and large trailers will have to forego the normal under-tree route and use the bypass road.

The Black Chamber is one of the severely burned Big Trees that tenaciously manage to hang on to life.

ABOVE A CANYON in the park's high country, Bearpaw Meadow trail camp occupies a breathtaking perch with a magnificent view. You can hike from here to the Big Trees grove in Redwood Meadow.

From the Crescent Meadow parking area, you can explore the Giant Forest area on foot, encircle the meadow—which was a favorite with John Muir—or walk out to Tharp's Log. This is a very unusual "cabin" made out of a fallen Big Tree, with a gable end, door, window, and stone fireplace added. It was the residence of Hale D. Tharp, the first white man to see the Big Trees of Sequoia National Park. He had a cattle camp in the area, and it is thought that he used the log for a summer home.

The fallen tree is 24 feet in diameter at the butt end and may have been nearly 300 feet tall when standing. The room inside is 56 feet long, eight feet high in front, and four feet high in the rear.

If you want to camp near the Big Trees of Giant Forest, look for a site in either Sunset Rock or Paradise campgrounds northwest of the main Giant Forest Lodge.

The view from Moro Rock

A well-surfaced, two-mile road from Giant Forest Village will take you to Moro Rock, a huge granite formation that towers more than 6,000 feet above the floor of the San Joaquin Valley. From the parking area, you can climb the 300 feet to the summit (there are guard rails and places to rest). The view from the top of the rock is one that no visitor to the park should miss. To the west are the low foothills of the Sierra, and beyond them the flat San Joaquin Valley. You see the canyons of the Kaweah River and its tributaries, and climaxing it all is the jagged crest of the Great Western Divide.

Redwood Meadow

This beautiful grove and meadow are accessible to camper-hikers who have three or four days to spend exploring the back country of Sequoia National Park. The grove is located near the upper end of the Middle Fork of the Kaweah River and is too far for a single day's hike from the Giant Forest Village area. Hikers usually walk into Bearpaw Meadow campground (about 11 miles from Crescent Meadow) and then explore the Redwood Meadow Big Trees on a shorter hike after a good night's rest.

Bearpaw Meadow is a trail camp for hikers and saddle horse parties. You don't have to carry anything into the camp, and you'll have a comfortable bed, a tent over your head, and one of the best views in the world for $5 a day, plus $2 or $3 per meal. Advance reservations are required.

IN PURSUIT OF THE BEAUTIFUL, THE TRUE AND THE GOOD

One of the oldest experiments in early California living was the ambitious but snakebitten Kaweah Colony that lived and died in the foothills below Giant Forest in the late nineteenth century. The whole thing was based on a Utopian dream that, if successful, would have created a great cooperative community, self-sufficient unto itself and a model for the whole world. However, it failed.

According to local history, the originators of the plan were J. J. Martin and B. F. Haskell of San Francisco and C. F. Keller of Traver. In 1885, these three Marx-inspired socialists and prominent leaders of early labor movements announced that an association something like a mutual company would be formed to acquire title to a large tract of timbered land in Tulare County. This land was along the North Fork of the Kaweah River and extended eastward across the Marble Fork.

Even though the government wanted to sell the land in small sections to separate buyers, Martin, Haskell, and Keller managed to file claims on all of it by rounding up applicants and giving each of them the $2.50 per acre that was necessary to file a claim. The land commissioner refused to accept the claims since most of them came from the same San Francisco address, but the buyers went ahead with their plans on the theory that their applications would have to be accepted eventually.

The Kaweah Cooperative Commonwealth Colony was organized to develop the land that was purchased and to start a lumbering enterprise. This association was intended to take care of its members through justice, fraternity, and cooperation, and to provide "a cultured, a scientific, an artistic life" for everyone. The organization set down a new creed of cooperation and universal brotherhood and vowed that "upon one of the flats by the river we shall build, out of the colored marble of Marble Canyon, a temple and a theatre for ourselves alone, and here also will be pursued the Beautiful, the True and the Good."

New members were invited, if they could put up $100 in cash and promise to donate another $400 in material or labor. Enough people were brought together so that a road into the timber was started near the end of 1886. Workers didn't get any money, but were paid in time checks at the rate of $2.40 a day. These checks supposedly could be saved and ultimately traded for other goods and services that the Colony generated.

The idea was so appealing to some folk that a town of Kaweah was formed about three miles above Three Rivers. It had about 100 homes, a planing mill, box factory, post office, company store, and newspaper. But troubles were soon coming. The Colony had some trouble keeping its books straight and frequently found itself short of cash. The members had plenty of time checks to cash, but the company store didn't have very much to offer in exchange. And since the time checks made very poor currency outside the Kaweah Colony, the colonists found themselves short of both money and material goods. There was plenty of grumbling and even a threat of open mutiny, but the organizers managed to keep the Commonwealth in operation for a few years.

By 1890 a 20-mile-long road into the mountains was completed, a sawmill was built, and the Colony had started to cut timber. But then the roof fell in. Congress created Sequoia National Park and included in it all of the lands of the Kaweah Cooperative Commonwealth Colony. All the claims of the colonists were denied and they were forced to leave. To further complicate matters, Martin and Haskell became enemies, the members fought among themselves, and the whole operation collapsed. By 1891, the Colony was disbanded and the Utopian dream was dissolved.

The original Kaweah post office can still be seen at the old town site, and the original Colony Mill Road built by the colonists still exists but is closed to traffic. Despite the failure of the Colony, it still deserves credit for building the first road into the Giant Forest and for attracting attention to the Big Trees. Maybe it wasn't Utopia, but Kaweah was the first home to some of California's most ambitious settlers.

ALL THAT REMAINS of Kaweah is its post office.

A FEW CABINS are all that remain of Mineral King. Elaborate winter sports facility is planned for area.

TROUT FISHERMEN often have good luck in Evelyn Lake, reached by trail from the Cold Spring area.

Mineral King Road

This road of 700 curves leads 25 slow miles into the old mining camp of Mineral King. The twisting, sporty drive is popular with many auto explorers, and it passes through and near a number of significant Big Tree groves.

You get your first look at the Big Trees along this road when you stop for the grand panoramic view at Lookout Point, just inside the Sequoia National Park boundary. As you look southwest across the canyon of the East Fork of the Kaweah River and up the forested sweep of Case Mountain, you can see the rounded crowns of mature Big Trees on the skyline more than two miles away. This is an isolated grove, outside of the park and far from any commercial development.

From this point on to Silver City, whenever the road swings out into the open to give you a view to the south beyond the river you will be able to spot Big Trees on the far slopes, in the swales and ravines, and even silhouetted on ridgetops.

After skirting a spectacular granite bluff just beyond Lookout Point, the road continues to wind up and away from the river. You come to the first close-up Big Trees, then to the site of old Atwell Mill, where logging began in 1879. Among the great stumps in the forest openings here, heavy machinery lies rusting in the grass, while symmetrical young Big Trees strive to replace their vanished elders. Chunks of the dark red wood of felled trees are still lying around, weathered but sound.

North of the road, a beautiful trail to the top of Paradise Ridge meanders easily up through the Skinner Grove, named for the Seattle preservationist who saved it from logging and then donated it to the national park

system. This grove contains one Big Tree growing at 8,800 feet, the highest in elevation to be found anywhere in the Sierra.

Across the road, the Atwell-Hockett Trail goes down from the Atwell Mill Campground and bridges a fine mossy section of the river gorge. A little way up the other side, you come to the extensive East Fork Grove of Big Trees, which is partly on national park lands and partly in Sequoia National Forest.

Garfield Grove

The Garfield Grove of Sequoia National Park and the Dillonwood Grove of Sequoia National Forest actually are two parts of the same grove that extends across Dennison Ridge. The whole forest embraces some 3,300 mature Big Trees and is one of the largest and most beautiful of all groves.

There is no way to drive into either half of the grove. From Three Rivers, you can drive to the South Fork Ranger Station and then hike three miles to the Garfield section. Approaching from the south, you can drive from Springville to Jack Flats Campground on a very steep road, and then walk along the old roadbed to the site of the Dillon Mill, which operated from 1875 to 1900. The partially cut Dillonwood section starts just north of the mill and climbs the slopes of Dennison Ridge. The logged area is particularly noted for its vigorous second-growth Big Trees.

The trees in this grove grow at elevations ranging from 3,000 to 8,000 feet. One lone tree growing below Clough's Cave along the South Fork of the Kaweah River is considered to be the lowest naturally growing Big Tree, at approximately 2,700 feet.

A FISHING FAMILY *tries for a trout dinner in one of the three man-made ponds (all stocked with trout) in Mountain Home State Forest and Balch Park. Balch Park Campground is located nearby.*

The Southern Sierra

There are more than a dozen groves of Big Trees on Sequoia National Forest lands south of Sequoia National Park. Five of them are readily accessible and large enough to warrant exploration. In addition, several thousand mature Big Trees are preserved in the Mountain Home State Forest and Balch County Park.

There are two good-sized groves of Big Trees on the Tule River Indian Reservation, but they are located on the main divide between the South Fork of the Tule River and adjacent drainages, and access is restricted to logging roads.

Mountain Home State Forest

This very scenic State Forest preserves about 4,500 acres of forest along the North Fork and the North Fork of the Middle Fork of the Tule River. Small areas were logged around the turn of the century and others in the 1940's before the acreage was purchased by the state, but more than 4,000 mature Big Trees are still standing.

Mountain Home is a managed forest. Much of the slash left over from the logging operations has been burned or cleared, and over-mature and diseased timber has been sold and cut. The open areas that lack natural reproduction have been planted with red fir and pine seedlings. There have been some experimental attempts at thinning and pruning the second-growth Big Trees to get rid of the second-rate saplings and allow the best trees to grow faster.

The selective logging and clearing has resulted in a great increase in natural reproduction of the trees, and has added to the enjoyment of the area by opening up scenic vistas. In some cases, all of the white fir has been cut out of the groves, so that the Big Trees have far less competition for light and nourishment and also stand out majestically for visitors to see. The results of such practices at Mountain Home have convinced some observers that similar efforts should be made in the national forests and parks.

The access road into Mountain Home State Forest leads right into the groves of Big Trees. There are excellent campsites—particularly at the Frasier Mill Campground—right under the Big Trees that have grown up since the mill quit operating in 1886. One of the most beautiful small stands of trees along the main road is

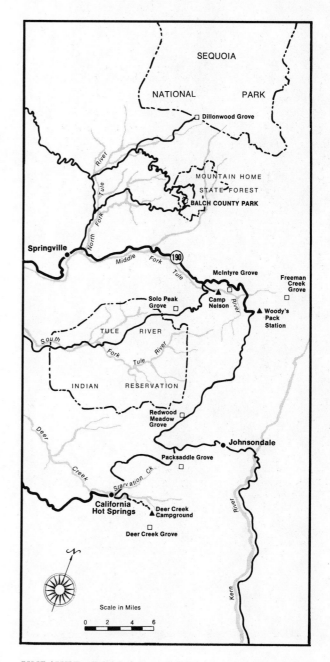

UNPAVED ROAD goes north from California Hot Springs, meets paved Great Western Divide Highway.

THERE ARE TADPOLES in the warm shallows of Balch Park pond. A young Big Tree stands at water's edge.

the Rosecrans Grove at the edge of Hedrick Pond.

The only other improved road in the State Forest is Summit Road, which circles through the forest east of the main visitor areas and provides access to Shake Camp Campground, a pack station, and Hidden Falls on the Middle Fork of the Tule. The Camp Lena Road connects Balch Park and Summit roads. You'll find several points of interest along this road, including the Centennial Stump, which is all that remains of one of the first Big Trees ever cut for exhibition. The tree was 111 feet in circumference and stood at least 300 feet high, according to unofficial reports. In 1877, entrepreneurs had it cut to make a traveling exhibit. Because the lumbermen didn't have the tools or the know-how to chop down such a giant (see page 71), the first cut was made 24 feet off the ground where the diameter was only 26 feet. The tall stump was hollowed out, cut into slabs and then reassembled with metal hinges when it went on exhibit. Despite some ambitious plans, the tree was displayed only at Visalia, Tulare and San Francisco.

The good loop trail that starts at Shake Camp takes you past the Adam Tree—the largest Big Tree in Mountain Home—and the Eve Tree, which was girdled and partially cut about 1900 but still stands. There are also some good examples of the rock basins or "Indian bathtubs" that are common to this area.

YOU CAN LOOK INSIDE Hercules Tree, a living Big Tree that was hollowed out between 1897 and 1902.

TILTED ROOTS of Big Tree cut before area became a park are a convenient perch for fisherman.

"INDIAN BATHTUBS" are found in Mountain Home State Forest. Exact origin and use of holes are unknown.

The strangest novelty along the Shake Camp Road is the Hercules Tree, which was hollowed out by an ambitious woodcutter between 1897 and 1902. He may have intended to live inside the tree, but the falling sap from the living wood made the den uninhabitable. However, in 1933, 31 campers took refuge in the clammy hole to escape the ravages of a violent windstorm that was felling trees on all sides. They spent two claustrophobic hours huddled inside the dark chamber while the world fell down around their ears, and emerged shaken but unscathed when the storm was over.

The stocky Methuselah Tree, next to the baseball diamond at the group campground just south of the forest headquarters, has the largest base circumference (96 feet) of any living Big Tree in Mountain Home.

Balch Park

Balch Park is a Tulare County park that is entirely enclosed within the boundaries of the Mountain Home State Forest. It contains about 200 mature Big Trees, some well-developed picnicking areas and campsites, and two glassy ponds that are good for trout fishing. Two of the best-known trees in Balch Park are the Lady Alice Tree, considered as one of the most beau-

A SHELTER for fur trappers and prospectors in 1800's, hollow log in Balch Park now amuses children.

DOUBLE-TRUNKED trees are not rare in the Sierra. This giant is in the Solo Peak Grove north of the Tule River Indian Reservation. You can explore the area on good dirt roads.

tiful of all the Big Trees, and a dead tree that was cut entirely through in 1897 but hasn't fallen over yet.

For those with more than a casual interest in the Big Trees, an excellent self-guiding nature trail starts at the county park headquarters and winds its way through the park and out into the Mountain Home State Forest, where some of the most interesting experiments in forest management are taking place.

Balch Park and the State Forest are generally open from the beginning of trout fishing season to the end of deer hunting season—the annual snowfall determines the actual opening and closing dates of the access roads.

McIntyre Grove

This big grove is easily accessible from State Route 190 through the Camp Nelson resort to Belknap Campground. Mature trees extend from Camp Nelson along both sides of the South Fork of the Middle Fork of

the Tule River all the way to Wheel Meadow. A good trail extends the full length of the grove (about three miles) so that campers stationed at Belknap can easily explore the area in one day.

Solo Peak Grove

Solo Peak Grove (formerly called Black Mountain Grove) is not the easiest stand of Big Trees to reach, but it is a joy to explore once you're on the scene. A good system of dirt roads winds among the trees, so you can see hundreds of beautiful mature trees before leaving your car. For those who want a closer look at the best specimens, the country is open and ideally suited for short—if sometimes steep—hikes.

The shortest route to Solo Peak is via the steep road from Camp Nelson (15 miles) on State Highway 190. You can also reach the grove from Porterville by climbing about 40 miles over a dirt road through the Tule

A SMALL CREEK runs alongside the base of this giant Big Tree in Solo Peak Grove. This grove has a large number of beautiful mature Big Trees and is a fine place for hiking.

River Indian Reservation. If you use this latter route, the first Big Trees you'll see are a half dozen large ones standing within sight of the road. As impressive as this small group might appear, it is a false front. The main part of the grove is still another mile up the road.

Solo Peak Grove covers about 1,700 acres on the divide that separates the streams flowing into the Middle and East forks of the Tule River. There are an estimated 1,000 mature Big Trees on the land, but motorists who take the time to explore the area slowly and carefully are likely to feel that there are twice that number.

Freeman Creek Grove

There are more than 500 mature Big Trees in Freeman Creek Grove, and they are magnificent specimens that are shown off to good advantage in a broad, forested basin on the Kern River watershed. The entire basin is in virgin condition, and a complete lack of roads keeps visitors to a minimum.

It is easy to see a few of the trees in Freeman Creek Grove, but some effort is required to see a lot of them. The head of the grove is less than a mile from Highway 190, and the main High Country trail heading east from the Quaking Aspen Meadow area cuts right across it. You can park at Woody's Pack Station (ask permission first) and pick up the trail just north of the corral. You'll be among the Big Trees after about 20 minutes of pleasant walking. The trees at this end of the grove are among the most magnificent in the entire basin.

To get into the main part of the grove, you'll have to leave the main trail where it crosses Freeman Creek and pick your way along the creek bed to the east. The range of the Big Trees extends along the tributaries at the west edge of the basin, and almost all of the really large trees are south of Freeman Creek.

REDWOOD MEADOW GROVE on Great Western Divide Highway is one of largest southern Sierra groves.

UNUSUAL CLUSTER of Big Trees probably developed when several seeds started in one patch of exposed soil.

Redwood Meadow

The red bark of the trees in Redwood Meadow can be startling to unsuspecting motorists who accidentally come across the grove as they drive along the curving Western Divide Highway. About two dozen mature specimens are quite close to the road, and they are a sharp change from the fir and pine forests that flank the highway for miles on either side.

There are a few trees east of the highway—including an unusual cluster of middle-aged trees that seem to have sprouted from the same square foot of soil—but the main part of this magnificent grove is west of the highway. It extends more than a mile to Horse Meadow Creek, and hikers can spend some enjoyable hours among the giants that cover the hillsides.

Packsaddle Grove

Packsaddle has about 350 mature trees, but they are not as concentrated as in some of the other groves in the southern Sierra. To see them all, you'll have to hike over a relatively large area. The grades are gradual for the most part, and an informal trail system links many of the best trees. The round crowns of the biggest trees are quite conspicuous on the skyline.

If you approach the Packsaddle Grove on the dirt road that leads north from the Pine Flat area, you'll drive just above a small grove of Big Trees down along Starvation Creek. You can see a few of the biggest trees from the road, but the main part of the grove is at the bottom of a steep ravine that defies easy hiking.

The main part of Packsaddle is easy to identify by the "Type I redwood grove" signs posted on roadside trees. If you start into the forest just behind one of these signs, you'll soon come across the Big Trees.

Deer Creek

Deer Creek is the southernmost grove of Big Trees in California. It is on a steep hillside above the small Deer Creek Mill Campground at the end of a dirt road east of Pine Flat. There are two mature trees right above the campground, and a few young specimens at the lower levels, but the major part of the grove is a 40-minute hike from the campground parking area. The most direct route from campground to Big Trees is the steep remnant of a skid road that was used to haul lumber during the early 1900's. A slightly longer, but much easier, alternate route veers to the right of the skid road and circles up to the grove on a more gradual grade.

The trail goes through an excellent stand of young trees about half an hour from the campground, and then the giants begin to show up on the neighboring slopes. Many tops are visible from the trail and the red bark shows up clearly through the fir and cedar. All 31 mature Big Trees are visible from the trail.

THE SOUTHERNMOST GROVE of Sierra Big Trees is the Deer Creek Grove on national forest land south of Sequoia National Park. The magnificent Big Trees in the grove tower above these two young hikers.

Index